A Garland Series

ROMANTIC CONTEXT: POETRY

Significant Minor Poetry
1789-1830

Printed in photo-facsimile
in 128 volumes

selected and arranged by
Donald H. Reiman
The Carl H. Pforzheimer Library

John Wilson Croker

*Familiar Epistles
to Frederick Jones, Esq.,*
On the Present State of the Irish Stage

The Amazoniad
or, Figure and Fashion

Histrionic Epistles

The Battles of Talavera

with an introduction
for the Garland edition by
Donald H. Reiman

Garland Publishing, Inc., New York & London

1979

Bibliographical note:

these facsimiles have been made from copies
in the Harvard University Library
Familiar Epistles;
The Newberry Library
The Amazoniad;
the Yale University Library
Histrionic Epistles;
and the University of Texas Library
The Battles of Talavera.

The volumes in this series have been printed on
acid-free, 250-year-life paper.

Library of Congress Cataloging in Publication Data

Croker, John Wilson, 1780-1857.
    Familiar epistles to Frederick Jones, Esq. ;
The Amazoniad ; Histrionic epistles ; The battles
of Talavera.

    (Romantic context : Poetry)
    Reprint of works published 1804-09, the first
of which was originally published under title:
Familiar epistles to Frederick J---s, Esq., on
the present state of the Irish stage.
    1.   Theater--Ireland--Poetry.   2.   Peninsular
War, 1807-1814--Poetry.   I.   Title.   II.   Series.
PR4518.C53F3   1979   821'.7   75-31188
ISBN 0-8240-2139-8

Introduction

John Wilson Croker (1780-1857) was born in Galway, Ireland, the son of an Irish civil servant. He was educated at Trinity College, Dublin, graduating 1800, and at Lincoln's Inn, London. Called to the Dublin bar in 1802, Croker dabbled in satirical poetry and prose before turning to politics. In 1807 Croker entered Parliament for Downpatrick, south of Belfast. He remained in London for the rest of his life, becoming, in turn, Secretary for Ireland in 1808 (assisting his friend and political ally Sir Arthur Wellesley, later Duke of Wellington), chief government spokesman in Parliament defending the Duke of York against the charges of Colonel Wardle (1809), and first Secretary of the Admiralty (1810 on) in which position he exposed a corrupt colleague and fought to restrict the independence of the Duke of Clarence, later King William IV.

Croker, a friend of Canning, began to contribute to the *Quarterly Review* by at least 1811. He remained a chief writer for the *Quarterly*, contributing about 270 articles on a multiplicity of subjects, sometimes writing several articles for a single issue. (The numbers for October 1815 and July 1816, for example, each contain four essays said to be his.) He became well known for the virulence of his literary reviews, which included notorious attacks on Keats's *Endymion* and Tennyson's *Poems* of 1832, as well as polemical articles from a militantly Tory perspective on such books as Lady Morgan's *France* and *Italy*. Croker and John Barrow, his junior colleague at the Admiralty Office, were the mainstays of the *Quarterly Review* during the editorship of William Gifford, and Croker continued to be the leading political voice in the *Quarterly* until 1854.

Southey and other contributors to the *Quarterly* tried to dissociate themselves from the harsh tone of Croker's attacks.

INTRODUCTION

Leigh Hunt lumped Gifford and Croker together as twin dark angels of the *Quarterly*. Thomas Moore (like Byron) maintained an acquaintance with Croker so that he could receive various favors conferred through Croker's twin power with the British navy and the *Quarterly Review*. When, after Moore's death, his private comments on Croker in his letters and journals showed how he despised the man, Croker was injudicious enough to publish Moore's letters to him, which showed the world how he had been used. Shelley seems to have been virtually unaware of Croker's existence, though he certainly read his *Quarterly* articles, including not unfavorable reviews of Godwin's *Mandeville* and Mary Shelley's *Frankenstein*.

Byron knew Croker well through Murray, Gifford, and the *Quarterly* group. But he made it a point, apparently, neither to become too friendly with him nor to offend him, because he respected the power of Croker's pen. In February 1814, when Byron was caught in the middle of a journalistic war involving R. C. Dallas and John Murray about the money and the copyrights for *Childe Harold*, *The Corsair*, and *The Bride of Abydos*, a satirical poem appeared in the Tory *Morning Post*. As Byron later explained to Murray, he was told that Croker was the author of this poem, and he wrote a sharp satire against Croker which—when the guess at authorship was contradicted—he destroyed. (These events, which seem never to have been explored by Byron scholars, can be inferred from Byron's letters to Moore, February 26, 1814, and to Murray, March 9, 1817.) Croker was one of the first to identify Byron as the author of *Beppo*, and he supplied John Gibson Lockhart with inside information on Byron and the Murray circle that Lockhart used to good advantage in *John Bull's Letter to Lord Byron* (1821; ed. A. L. Strout, 1947), a work of criticism and raillery admired by both Byron and twentieth-century scholars.

William Hazlitt, who like Hunt despised Croker on political grounds, alludes to Croker frequently in his writing, at least

INTRODUCTION

twice mentioning Richard Cumberland's characterization of the young John Wilson Croker as a "talking potatoe." Croker plays a prominent role (along with George Croly) in Hazlitt's dialogue-essay "On Envy" in *The Plain Speaker* (1826). N(orthcote) and H(azlitt) discuss different forms of envy, and both speakers use Croker as an example, Northcote describing his disparagement of painting and painters (including Raphael) at a dinner of the Royal Academy and Hazlitt excoriating Croker's caricature drawing of Napoleon (Hazlitt, *Complete Works*, ed. P. P. Howe, XII, 100-101). In *The Spirit of the Age*, Hazlitt's essay on "Mr. Gifford" alludes to Croker (correctly) as the *Quarterly*'s reviewer of books on Napoleon at St. Helena. Here Croker touched a sore spot in Hazlitt's feelings, for of all the major British writers of the age, Hazlitt alone consistently venerated Bonaparte.

But Croker himself, in his poem on *The Battles of Talavera*, honors the prowess of the French . . . if only to enhance his praise of Sir Arthur Wellesley. Napoleon himself was not present in Spain at the time, and Croker, in a note on page 35, admits that he "has never ventured to indulge any very sanguine hope of the final success of the Spanish cause," pointing to parallels in the War of the Spanish Succession, which ended in partial victory for the France of Louis XIV. Croker's poem is clever propaganda for his friend Wellesley as well as for the government's war policy. But though its poetic merit is limited, Croker's poem shows that he possessed considerable rhetorical skill. Unlike George Croly, Croker does not diminish the achievement of his heroes by denigrating their antagonists. He exhibits magnanimity and stresses that the British-Spanish victory was achieved through the foresight and energy of Wellesley and the courage of his troops, rather than because of stupidity or cowardice on the part of the French. Moreover, Croker exhibits considerable mastery of versification and diction appropriate to his purpose—as he does also in his Dublin satirical poems. Croker's motives may have been despicable, but as Byron

vii

INTRODUCTION

recognized, his energy and his intellectual powers were
not.

Croker's political philosophy undoubtedly sprang from his
peculiar socioeconomic background. The son of an excise
officer, he himself spent almost his entire adult life as a
government official, and he was dependent upon his role as a
public servant for even his original appointment as a
Quarterly reviewer. Croker was a leading parliamentary
opponent of electoral reform, and he refused to sit in
Parliament after the passage of the Reform Bill of 1832. He
and others in his position remained the staunchest, most
uncompromising supporters of the political *status quo* because
change threatened their entire economic base. The government
officials in Great Britain had become, by the middle of the
eighteenth century, the real rulers of the country, holding the
balance of power between the nation's agricultural and
industrial interests and controlling vast economic power in the
form of government sinecures and other lucrative political
appointments both within Britain and in exploitable colonies
such as India. Croker, as an official and as a writer, was thus the
enemy of all writers who advocated a more equitable
distribution of political power or wealth, of all who opposed
wars to acquire or to defend colonies, of all who advocated
government promotions by merit or service to all the people
rather than self-perpetuating government by those who
agreed to share proportionately in the spoils of office. In the
1830s Croker battled against Thomas Babington Macaulay's
Whiggish interpretation of history. He was the unchanging
child and champion of one age and lived to become the hated
and despised reactionary of the next. There is no doubt,
however, that as both writer and political touchstone, Croker
played an important part in the context of Romantic poetry in
Great Britain. (For further information, see *The Croker
Papers*, ed. L. J. Jennings [3 vols., 1884], and M. F. Brightfield,
John Wilson Croker [1940].)

Donald H. Reiman

Familiar Epistles

TO

FREDERICK J——S, ESQ.

ON THE

PRESENT STATE

OF THE

IRISH STAGE.

Vererer ne immodicam hanc epiſtolam putares niſi
eſſet generis ejus, ut ſæpe incipere ſæpe deſinere videa-
tur: nam ſingulis criminibus, ſingulæ velut cauſæ con-
tinentur.

PLIN. Epiſt. ad Macrin.

Faciendo profeſſione di candida verità parlerò ſenz'
amore e ſenz' odio di ciaſcheduno.

DAVANZ. Stor. Rom.

Dublin:

JOHN BARLOW, BOLTON-STREET.

1804.

I SHOULD be almoſt aſhamed to de-
dicate the following trifle to any one ;
but if the ſubject and execution were of
more importance, and greater excellence, I ſhould not heſitate to inſcribe
it to HIM,—in whoſe family the titles
of his nobility have been even leſs hereditary, than the learning and the
taſte of the ſcholar and the gentleman,
to—LORD HARDWICKE.

A 2   *T. C. D.*

PREFACE.

THE following letters are the hasty* effusions
of my holy-day leisure, and originally aspired
to no higher rank in the literary world, than a
place in the public papers; but after some tri-
als, I found, that the Dublin Editors and Mr.
Jones, had sworn an inviolable friendship, and

A 3   that

---

* The verse was written within as many days as
there are letters: *this* is no excuse for their incorrectness,
but the kind of publication for which they were intended, is.—Besides my avocations do not allow me leisure
for revision; he therefore, who cannot forg've harsh
metre, and rambling meaning, had better read no further—if he does, let him not then blame me; he has
had fair warning.

that no effay in which his name was mentioned,
would be inferted " fans fon aveu.—"

I really have no very exalted opinion of the merit of my verfes, I know them, "tenui effe oratione
et fcripturâ levi," yct I am vain enough to
hope, that they may be worth a fhilling or two,
(were it only to laugh at) and therefore I prefent them to thofe, who have a fhilling to throw
away, in the only fhape in which it is, in Ireland, poffible to publifh them.

To my *readers* (for I fuppofe they will be,
vel *duo* vel nemo) I can only promife, that tho'
they may not be much amufed by my rhymes,
they fhall at leaft be exercifed in fome of the
moral virtues ; for befides the generofity of giv-
ing the poor bookfeller a fhilling for what is
perhaps not worth a farthing, they will alfo
have to applaud themfelves for much patience
and long fuffering ;—and as a fpecimen, I beg
leave to detain them, while I give fome account

count of the occasion and object of a work, which they perhaps, have already resolved never to read.

The management of a private theatre, the temple of the folly, or as some have (I believe falsely) said, of the vice of a few individuals, who had more money than wit,* and more leisure than either, was the first dramatic exercitation of our present Patentee, and it is said that he acquitted himself most meritoriously in this important office ; so resplendent at least, were his ministerial talents in the eyes of the judicious subscribers to this puppet-show, that they were easily led to believe that no other person was half so well qualified to be the *arbiter elegantiarum* of the kingdom.

They therefore zealously laboured to procure for Mr. Jones, the reversion of the patent

* Some of them to do them justice, were less deficient in wit than in sense.

tent which Daly then held, or at leaft, a licence to open a fecond theatre in Dublin.
The Lord Lieutenant was foon fubdued into fomething like a promife, and Daly to
fave himfelf from the threatening ftorm, was
obliged to make terms * with, and abdicate
his throne in favour of the conquering Jones.

This, it muft be confeffed, was to the public
a matter of much fatisfaction.   Daly had long
fince, either by negligence or incapacity, diffa-
tisfied the Citizens of Dublin, and the elegant
and liberal tafte of the new Proprietor was
every where extolled by fome who knew him,
and by many more who did not ; and thus with
a pretty general approbation, he obtained a
                                                    defpotic

* It is much to Mr. Jones's credit, that he gave Daly his own terms; this was *genercus* and it was juft,
confidering the fituation to which Daly's property had
been reduced.

despotic monopoly of the Theatres Royal of *Cork, Limerick* and *Dublin.*

What the annual profits of this monopoly may be, it is impossible for *me* to affect ; but I have heard them estimated by *well-informed* persons, at a sum † more than the salary of two of the judges of the land!!!

I am always pleased at the honest good fortune of any man, and therefore I rejoice at Mr. Jones's most extraordinary success ; but then, I should hope, it were not unreasonable to expect, that the single company to which all the dramatic expence of a generous people is tributary, should, in return for such exclusive patronage, display all the variety and excellence of which such an establishment is capable.

Whether it is so conducted,—what has been done towards encouraging humble merit and securing the *permanent* assistance of acknowledged

† More than 5000l. per annum.

ledged abilities,—and generally the prefent ftate of the public amufements of the capital, are the principal objects of the following enquiry.

If we were to fubmit our judgment to that of the public papers, the caufe would foon be decided :—Thofe impartial Chronicles will af- fure us, that fo far from deferving cenfure, the conduct of the theatre,—the felection of per- formances,—and the choice and abilities of the actors,* are all intitled to the moft implicit and unqualified approbation.

But whatever refpect we may have for the opinions of fome of the very ingenious perfons who act as the Editors of newfpapers, we are not bound to give the flighteft credence to thofe

dramatic

---

* The Lord Polonius was a very niggard of com- mendation, *au prix*, of thefe journals. " The beft actors in the world, either for tragedy, comedy, hifto- ry, paftoral, paftoral-comical, hiftorical-paftoral, tragi- cal-hiftorical, tragical-comical, hiftorical-paftoral, fcene individable, or poem unlimited,"—*Hamlet*.

dramatic criticisms, which every journalist so plentifully admits into his columns, and for the truth of which venal * advertisements, and paid-for puffs, he is, in fact, no more responsible, than for the cheapness and excellence of each article in Twigg's repository, or Percy's auction-rooms.

We cannot justly blame them for inserting whatever they are paid † to insert—'tis their trade

---

* Falstaffe was desirous of knowing " where a commodity of *good names* were to be *bought* ;" poor Sir John ! did he live in our time, he might easily buy courage, honour and generosity, temperance, soberness, and chastity, for less than a gallon of sack. So generally are " omnia venalia," that I should not be surprised to hear some sagacious disquisitor assert, that— I was a *hired* scribbler.—And really if I cared about *such* reputation as the world now-a-days bestows, I should follow the example of Stesichorus, and never write of a *living* creature. πεφύλαξαι μὲν οὖν, says Phalaris to him, γράφειν εἰς τὰς κατὰ σεαυτον ανθρώπυς ἱνα μὴ δοξῃ σὺ τὶς ὠνίαν εἶναι τὴν ποςὸσιν.

† Mais faudra-t-il pour leur plaire renoncer au sens commun? faudra-t-il applaudir indifféremment à toutes

les

trade and even their duty : as well might we complain of their reprefenting a horfe as found, or a poft-chaife as good as new, when in truth the fteed is foundered, and the carriage in pieces.—God forbid that I fhould expect from newfpapers, nothing but plain fenfe and honeft truth—I am not fo unreafonable.

> Ecrive donc qui voudra, chacun à ce métier,
> Peut perdre impunément de l'encre et du papier.

But whilft we read thefe effufions, let us always recollect that it is the *actor* that gravely defcants on *his own* fpirited performance, or the *fiddler* † that modeftly extols the brilliancy of *his own* tafte, and the fkill of *his own* execution ! ! !

Thus

les impertinences qu'un ridicule aura répandues fur le papier ? Boil. Difc. fur la Satyre.

† A whimfical inftance of this " ηχοὶ χαλχος" this *mufical brafs* occurs to me, and I fhall give it as a fpe-cimen; in one of the late papers (I believe the Free-man's

Thus much I think it neceffary to fay in my own defence, for rejecting, *as I altogether do,* the evidence of the newfpapers, on the fubject under confideration.

Let me now fay a few words on the ftyle and matter of thefe epiftles :

Were that an *eafy ftyle* which is eafily written,* I fhould have no paternal fears of the fuccefs of this little book. We, fubalterns of poetry, fhould foon become the field officers, and no one

B who

man's Journal) an admirable piece of theatrical criti-cifm, replete with Horatian judgment, and Addifonian graces, concluded its account of the mufical performance with this elegant idea, " and tho' there are *two Cookes* in the orcheftra, we cannot fay that they *fpoil the broth*" ! ! ! This is *very kitchenftuff!*

* " It is a curious illuftration" fays the *Editor* of Mr. Little's poems, " of the labour which fimplicity re-quires, that the Ramblers, elaborate as they appear,

were

who had the infolence to take any pains with
his appearance, would be permitted to fhow
himfelf on the parade of a bookfeller's counter,
but unhappily this regulation has not yet taken
place, and an ill judging world ftill throws in
our teeth

 You write with eafe to fhow your breeding,
 But *eafy* writing 's damn'd *hard* reading.

          On

were written with fluency, and feldom required revifi-
on; while the fimple language of Rouffeau, which feems
to come flowing from the heart, was the flow production
of painful labour, paufing on every word, and ballan-
cing every fentence." The verfe of Mr. Little himfelf,
eafy and light as it feems, is faid to have been wrought
with very much of the " limæ labor & mora." I could
wifh his fentiments were but half as correct as his verfi-
fication; but the only Venus he worfhips, is fhe whom
the Scholiaft on Ariftophanes calls Γενετυλλις, and what
is worfe, he makes all the young people in the Empire,
worfhip her too. I recommend to Mr. Little's confideration, (for I am told he is ftill alive, and ftill an author)
          the

On this topic then, gentle reader, I have only to refer you to my title page, in which you will find my gracious permiſſion to throw down my book when ever it ſhall tire you, and take it up again, when you have nothing elſe to do.

And now of the *matter* ;—

No one I believe will ſay, that profeſſing to treat of plays and play-houſes, I ſhould, or indeed *could* have refrained from mentioning the players, unleſs he be ſuch a caſuiſt as Mr. Shandy, who, being bound by his marriage articles to keep a coach, aſſerted, that he was not thereby obliged to provide horſes to draw it—what

B 2 horſes

the precept of one of the beſt poets the modern world has produced :

Un auteur vertueux dans ſes vers innocens
Ne *corrompt* point le *cœur*, en *chatouillant* les *ſens:*
Son feu n'allume point de *criminelle flame.*
Aimez donc la vertu, nourriſſez-en votre ame ;
En vain l'eſprit eſt plein d'un noble vigeur,
Le vers ſe ſent toujours des baſſeſſes du *cœur.*

horfes are to a coach, actors are, I humbly conceive, to a theatre ; and this I imagine will be a
fufficient apology for the freedom I take, in confidering their merits and imperfections. I hope
I fhall not be found a very ill-natured cenfor—I
have ftudioufly avoided all fevere allufions to
private character, and have rather inclined to the
* equity of mercy, than to the rigor of fatire ;
but

> Si quis eft, qui dictum in fe inclementius
> Exiftimat effe, fic exiftimet—
> Refponfum non *ita* dictum

that it has not been faid with an intention to offend, but becaufe *truth* " lay in my way, and
I found it."

Every other perfon that I have alluded to, is
alfo, *publici juris*, either from his ftation or character,

* Quando pudiere, y deviere tener lugar la *equidad*,
no cargues todo il rigor de la *fatyrà* al delinquinte.
Cervant.

racter, and will be so good as to remember that a liberty to praise or censure, is a privilege which an inhabitant of a free country always exacts from *notoriety*.

One word more to the Patentee, and I have done.

Let me assure him, that so far from having any hostile intentions towards him, I like and esteem him, as a pleasant companion, and an honourable gentleman, and I dare say he will easily perceive that my advice and criticism, are not those of an enemy. His management of the Theatre, has been in many instances extremely injudicious : the total want of great, the small number of respectable, and the dismal herd of indifferent actors, are evident and inexcusable—the choice of plays is frequently of an indiscrimination, only to be equalled by the cast of the characters, and a total inattention to the production of Irish abilities, either active or graphic, is a source of concern to every friend of the drama, of literature, and of Ireland.

But

But againſt theſe errors and omiſſions, much propriety and decency * of regulation, much ſplendor of decoration, much punctuality with thoſe in his employment, and much readineſs to adopt, *what he thinks*, good advice are to be ballanced—wiſhing therefore, that henceforward there may be larger opportunities for com-mendation, and leſs neceſſity for cenſure, I ſhall make

* Much however remains to be done, tho' indeed it is difficult to ſay how it is to be accompliſhed, or by what means the theatre can be kept ſacred from the li-bertiniſm and drunkenneſs, which now ſo often invade it, under the very eyes of our wives and daughters.

Spectant hoc nuptæ, juxta recubante marito
Quod pudeat *narraſſe* aliquem præſentibus ipſis.

Juv.

The Grecian theatres, ſays Lactantius (l. 6.) were de-dicated to *Bacchus* and *Venus*. If ſome exertion is not made by the well diſpoſed part of the community, *ours* will ſoon become ſo too, and not metaphorically. I *know* that Mr. Jones, on this ſubject, thinks as I do, and I hope he will deviſe ſome means of preventing the growth of ſo tremendous an evil.

make my parting compliment to him in the
words of a monarch of Antiquity, ουδὲν ἄχαρὶ
βύλομαι σε παθεῖν ἀπ᾽ ἐμῦ, πλέιω γαρ ευρίσκω σοι τὰ
ἀγαθὰ πεπραγμένα, των χειρονων. διὸ καὶ τῦτὸ σὖ τῶν
βελτιόνων ἕν γενέσθω, τὸ μὴ προσαναγκάσαι με, τῳ
καλεπωτέρῳ τησ ψυχης κατα σὖ χρησασθαι παθει.*

Jan. 10, 1804.

* Φαλαρ. επιτολ. Νεολαΐδα.

TO

FREDERICK J——S, Esq.

PATENTEE

OF THE

THEATRE ROYAL.

—————

FIRST EPISTLE.

—————

Tu, quid ego, et populus mecum defideret, audi.
HOR. A. P.

—————

J——S*, who directs with equal skill
The bill of fare, and play-houfe bill,
Whofe tafte all other palates fways
Either in difhes, or in plays,

And

* J——s. To fuch of my readers as have the misfortune not to belong to Daly's, or be in habits of eating with
the bon vivants of Dublin, it may be neceffary to fay,
that Mr. J——s underftands the regulation of a table

B   at

And rightly judges where there should
Come *entremets* or interlude;
Whose genius never at a lofs is
Either for farces, or for fauces,
And regulates with happieft care
An epilogue or a *deffert*.
You, who with equal judgment fit
The arbiter of wine and wit,
By palate and by patent plac'd
Upon the *double* throne of tafte;
If you, dear manager, can fpare a
Moment from Turbot and Madeira,
You'll find perhaps that my epiftle,
Tho' not fo fweet to mouth or whiftle,
And flat, in edible refpe& ,
Is favoury to the intelle&.

For I would feek the wond'rous caufe,
That abrogates our ancient laws,

And

at leaft as well as that of a theatre; which is not fur-
prifing, when we confider how much more the former has employed his thoughts and his time.

And like the Gallic revolution,
Subverts old Crow-ftreet's conftitution ;
Thus Shakefpeare, Monarch of the realm
Of plays, his fubjeĉts overwhelm,
And mad with rebel fury grown,
Infult, and fentence, and dethrone ;—
Thus Fletcher, Jonfon, Otway, Rowe,
The nobles of the ftage, are low,
Or elfe difpers'd by barbarous arts,
Are * *émigrés* in foreign parts;
Whilft in their places rife and fit,
The very *tiers-etat* of wit ;
And high o'er all in tragic rage
† Kotzebue, chief conful of the ftage ;
B 2

Of

* Our old Englifh authors however defpifed at home,
are in high requeft abroad, and afford indeed a very
ample fund to the French and German plagaries.

† Without having any great refpeĉt for Kotzebue's
moral charaĉter, it is but juftice to declare, that it is
only in his dramatic capacity that I compare him with
the worft man of this, or perhaps of any age.

Of lineage foreign and obfcure,

Of manners harfh, of thought impure;

Bold, brutal, bloody, and in few,

Juft like his brother of St. Cloud.

In managers, the ftage and ftate

Have to lament as hard a fate;—

'Tis no more Barry, or Choifeul,

Fleuri, or Sheridan, that rule,

But Talleyrand and J——s * appear,

And Fouché there, and F-ll-m * here.

But with comparifons a truce—

What is our manager's excufe ?

B 2   What

* J——s, F-ll-m. Far be it from me to put thofe
refpectable gentlemen, in the fame rank with the *apof-
tate Talleyrand*, or the *Septembrifer Fouché*, in any
other than a metaphorical fenfe; they are the minif-
ters of a *revolutionized ftage*; as fuch I diflike and op-
pofe their adminiftration : But very unlike other oppo-
fitionifts, I may be brought over by a change of mea-
fures, without a change of men.—If Mr. Windham
reads this note, he will pronounce me an egregious
blockhead,

What can he urge in his defence,

For want of judgment and of fenfe ?

" He owns," he fays, " the ancient plays

" Are feldom acted now a days,

" And modern critics rather choofe

" A younger than a grandam mufe ;

" That 'tis his bufinefs to provide

" For people's taftes and not to guide,

" And with the nice and fqueamifh town,

" That novelties alone go down."

But can we not *ourfelves* produce

Thefe novelties for Irifh ufe,

That we to foreign hands muft roam,

For goods we us'd to make at home ?

Where is the foul of drama fled ?

Is genius paralyz'd or dead ?

That artlefs Southerne's* native fhore,

Produces tragic bards no more.

B 3

Shall

* Divini ingegni, i quali coi lor belliffimi penfieri e nobliffimi opere la patria ed età loro adornavano. Tolom: Oraz.

And fhall we never fee their like again ?—

Shall Farquhar's, Congreve's, native ifle
No more with wit peculiar fmile?
And can no kindred foul, from death,
Catch Sheridan's expiring breath,
And give the ftage, for one life more,
A leafe of humour's choiceft ftore?
Does time with niggard hand infpire
Our later age with feebler fire?
Or is it that dramatic genius
In Ireland's a crime fo heinous,
That no man durft prefume to fhow it
Either as player or as poet?—
Heaven ne'er inflicts a *mental* blight
On *all* abilities outright;
The rain and wind will ruin corn,
But what can mildew wit unborn,
And blaft like barley, wheat or bere
Genius " en ventre de fa mere."
How comes it then that 'tis by rumour
Alone, we know of Irifh humour,

And

And our dramatic talent all is

Comprized in Atk——on * and La——efs? †—

Poor Atk——on, kind hearted creature,

Soul of good humour and good nature,

Whofe inoffenfive gabble runs

Eternal, with eternal puns,

But fit to write a play, no more

Than J——b P——le, ‡ or Lord Gl——ore. §

L——efs

* Atk——on. Jofeph Atk——on, Efq. M. R. I. A. &c. &c. author of " Love in a Blaze," an operatical drama, a ftrange collection of ftupid, and fometimes indecent vulgarifms, upon which Sir John Stevenfon threw away fome very good mufic, which it had coft him much trouble to *compile*. " a cctte mervielle la, plus d'un fpectateur bailla."

† L——lefs, the author of " Trial's All,"a comedy, produced not long finee at Crow-ftreet. If I remember rightly, the plot was, that a young man, accufed of a confpiracy, is brought to trial and acquitted; *what could have turned Mr. L——lefs's cogitations to fuch Green-ftreet fubjects ?*

‡ J——b P——le, our late Lord M——r, a citizen of pretorian activity and critical acumen.

' § Lord Gl——ore. I am told that this noble Peer

is

La——efs indeed I own is not

Unfit to carry on a *plot*, *

And, as we're ready to confefs,

Preferves the *unities* t' excefs;

But for the reft,—the glowing mind,

Terfe thought, and dialogue refined;

He'll do our country as much honour

As Nelfon, Ruffel, or O'Connor.

Unhappy Dowling! † on your head

The crimes of other men were fhed,

And

is a fcholar and a man of parts; fhall I venture to own,
I never could difcover in him any refemblance to either.
He would make a good Lord of the bed-chamber, but
for any thing elfe—!!!

* Can thefe mean *play-houfe* plots and unities?

† Dowling. This perfon from being a brazier, me-
tamorphofed himfelf into a very middling painter, and
finally became an indifferent actor, under the title of
Mr. Herbert.—He fathered L——lefs's play, which before reprefentation was extolled as a miracle of genius,
but alas! " Trial's All"—the piece was not fo fortunate
as its hero. I do not forget to Mr. D——ing, the play

he

And prudent L——lefs heard fecur'd
The hearty hifs that you endur'd,
Whilft in your fecret foul you thought
'T were better hammer pan or pot
Or e'en with hireling pencil trace,
G——n's * fhape, or K—x's * face,
Than hope to rife to wealth or fame,
By father'd play and borrow'd name.

But fome aver that the defeЄ
Springs from the manager's negleЄ ;
" For who of common fenfe," they fay,
" Would *write* what there are none to *play,*
" Or venture to entruft his pieces
" To fuch a company as this is,
" Who

he chofe for his benefit in a time of fedition and Jaco-
binifm :—But as he has ceafed to refide among us, it is
of no confequence to enquire into his political principles.

* G——n, K—x. Had thefe gentlemen not been
often publicly affured that they were not beauties, I
fhould not have prefumed to have made them the *au
pis aller,* of a painter's averfion.

" Who feem with equal ſkill to handle

" *Lock and Key*, and *School for Scandal*.

" Holman † may carry to our neighbours

" Of Drury Lane, his Iriſh labours,

" And M——e, * with Coleman's aid evince

" His geniu₃ in the *Gipſey Prince*,

" But bards in gen'ral would be undone

" By the mere journey up to London.

" And thus in Iriſh durance pent,

" The brighteſt mind muſt be content

" To

† Holman is now in London, foliciting the acceptation of a piece, written during his ſtay in Ireland.

* M——e. Tommy M——e. In Ireland we uſed to ſhow our admiration of his poetic talents, by aſking him to ſupper ; in England they reward him with a commercial, and in ſome degree legal office—this ſhews the difference of the national taſte ;—with us, abilities are diſſipated in conviviality, and with them, fettered by the ties of intereſt and buſineſs. Between us, I fancy poor Tom is not likely to be much improved, or *even enriched.*

" To fee our *thefpian murderers maul

" His fcenes, or elfe not write at all."—

This cenfure, whether falfe or juft,

Cannot at prefent be difcufs'd,

But if I find, you take not this ill

I'll weigh it in my next epiftle.

SECOND

* In fuch hands, if any perfon were mad enough
to write for the Irifh ftage, I fancy we might fay with
the French Vaudville :

Tandis que l'un tombe fur l'or,

   L'autre tombe dans la mifère ;

Rarement on tombe d'accord,

   Beaucoup tombent dans la rivière.

On voit quelquefois un amant

   Tomber au genoux de fes belles ;

Mais ce qui tombe très fouvent,

   Ce font nos *pièces nouvelles.*

SECOND EPISTLE.

———————

Mimæ balatrones hoc genus omne
Mæſtum ac Sollicitum eſt :   HOR. L. 1. S. 2.

———————

A flouriſh, trumpets! beat ye drums,
The Crow-ſtreet corps in triumph comes,
Fierce in theatric pride, they take
The hoſtile field for glory's ſake,
To vindicate before the town
Their maſter's honour and their own ;
And prove to viſual demonſtration,
The juſtice of their reputation.
In perſon every gallant ſoul
That nightly drains the tragic bowl ;
And all who in the comic ſtrife
Kick up their heels and call it life ;
And every ſon of farce, and all
Whŏ op'ras ſcrape, or op'ras ſquall,

                                        Each

Each Leap-Jack that thro' ballets capers,
And all who light and snuff the tapers :
And laft, not leaft, the houfehold troops,
Rally around their chief in groups,
Eager for fight ;—the heroes brandifh
Their fwords, the box-keeper his ftandifh,
The tribe of *Shuffletons* * their fwitches,—
Their truncheons ghofts,—their brooms the witches :—
The Mechanifts † in dire commotion
With ftorms difturb the earth and ocean,

C   Blow

* The *tribe* of Shuffletons, becaufe the authors and
(where they have omitted it) the actors have, of late,
reprefented all young men of rank or vivacity, with
a moft difgufting famenefs of vulgarity, folly and vice.
—" facies omnibus una."

† Mechanifts. I put thofe gentlemen in the higheft
place of my climax, becaufe really their *éleves*, the fea,
the rocks, the trees, and the tempefts, are the moft admired, and indeed the beft performers we have. I have
more than once feen an unruly audience entirely appeaf-
ed by a thunder-ftorm ; and a well timed fhower of
rain never fails (if fufficiently violent) to produce the
moft comfortable, and tranquillizing effects.

Blow up their mines, burft rocks in funder,
And roll, like Jove of yore, the thunder.

" Reft, reft, perturbed fpirits reft ;"
Smooth the brow, and calm the breaft :
Vain is your buftle, and your fear
Caufelefs, no enemy is near.

Mean is the foul whofe four chagrin,
Private hate, or caufelefs fpleen,
Aims to wound with felon dart,
The feelings of the honeft heart—
But juft as much I loath the mind
Whom private intereft can bind :
And who with mercenary aim,
Scatters around promifcuous fame,—
Equals to Garrick or to Barry
The Hero * of the pufh and parry ;

Difcreetly

* A very good fencing mafter *perhaps*, a very indifferent player moft certainly. If Bonaparte ever obtains
the dominion of the Irifh republic, I hope he will not
have the ingratitude to forget him who fo pompoufly
difplayed

Difcreetly hints that fportive Clive

In Da—d—n † is ftill alive :

Or with more fhamelefs puff will tell ye

That C—ke ‡ is equal to Correlli.

Far, far from thefe my courfe is drawn

Averfe to flander, or to fawn.

C 2   To

difplayed the triumphs of Marengo, in the very Theatre *Royal* of the Capital.—Mr. J——s, Mr. J——s,
you permitted it ! Is not your name in the red-book,
Mr. J——s, as one of the Viceroy's houfehold ?

† Da—d—n. I pity this poor girl, who is for ever
obtruded on the public in parts very unfit for her ; fhe
may, for aught I know, have her own little merits, but
they muft be in a very different ftyle of character from
that fhe ufually plays.

‡ C—ke. The modeft and diffident Mr. T. C—ke,
who played on eight different inftruments for his *own*
benefit ;—I am fure it was neither benefit or pleafure to
any one elfe. This perfon writes *new* overtures, to all
the operas which are imported to our ftage, beginning
generally

To actor I have never fpoken,

Nor feen a play on actor's token :

By them ne'er mimick'd or abufed,

Nor granted orders * or refufed ;

I've no temptation, thanks to fate,

To private love or private hate.

Come then, dear J——s, as Colonels ufe

T' attend the gen'ral that reviews,

" Bear" by my fide, " a wary eye,"

And fee your regiment march by.

First

generally with *chords*, and ending with an Irifh *jig*, and this he calls *compofition*. The young man however has fome merit, and if he went to London, would probably make two or three guineas a week by playing country dances at the winter balls.—Serioufly, I wifh he could be taught a little fcience, a little tafte, and a little modefty, and he might be a very ufeful and agreeable fiddler.

* Orders, in theatrical language, mean free admiffions, with which actors fometimes gratify their friends; tho' I am told they generally expect fome remuneration, either in the difpofal of tickets for their benefits, or the inditing puffs for the public prints. *Damufque, petimuf-que.*——

Firſt T—lb—t † comes, the firſt indeed—

But fated never to ſucceed

In the diſcerning eye of thoſe

Who form their taſte on Kemble's noſe,

And deem that genius a dead loſs is

Without dark brows, and long probofcis ;

T—lb—t, 'tis certain, muſt deſpair

To rival Kemble's fombrous ſtare,

Or reach that quinteſſence of charms

With which black Roſcius moves his arms.

A trifling air and girliſh form,

Ill fitted to the tragic ſtorm :

A baby face, that ſometimes ſhows

Alike in tranſports or in woes,

Will ne'er permit him to reſemble,

Or ſoar the tragic flights of Kemble ;

C 3

Yet

† T—lb—t. Tho' I have ſo fully given my opinion of T—lb—t in verſe, let me however add in proſe, that I fear he is not quite ſo great a favourite behind the curtain, as he is before it.—I ſhould wiſh to ſee him oftener.

Yet in fome * fcenes together plac'd

His greater feeling, equal tafte

From a judicious audience draws

As much and as deferv'd applaufe.

But whatfoe'er his tragic claim,

He rules o'er comedy, fupreme, †

And fhows by nature chaftly fit

To play the gentleman or wit;

Not Harris's, nor Coleman's boards,

Nor all that Drury-lane affords,

Can paint the rakifh Charles ‡ fo well,

Give fo much life to ‡ Mirabel;

Or fhow for light and airy fport,

So exquifite a ‡ Doricourt.

Sometimes

* Tullus Aufidius in Coriolanus, **and Lifimachus in** Alexander (amongft many other **of his parts) are** fine fpecimens of his ability—**whether it arifes from emula-** tion or chance, I cannot determine **; but he certainly** plays beft, when he plays with Kemble.

† Let me not be underftood to reprefent **T-lb-t as a** *perfect* comic actor, when I only confider him, **as the** leaft diftant from excellence, of any that I have *lately* feen.—Proximus, fed *intervallo*.

‡ Charles, Mirabel, and Doricourt. **I have feen him**
play,

Sometimes it feems that thoughts arife,
That cloud his brow, and dim his eyes,—
Buried be fuch within his breaft
There whilft he's acting let them reft;
Nor on his countenance be fhown,
Whining mirth and maudlin fun;—
Nor let him, negligent of grace,
Swing his arms and writhe his face,
Nor fway and balance with his form,
Like failors walking in a ftorm;
But move the courfe, by Garrick * track'd, in,
And act—as if he were not acting;—
So every tedious ordeal paffed,
Fortune *muft* Crown his toils at laft.

Away—for fad G-li-do room—!
Living memento of the tomb;—
Upon her dark unalter'd brow,
Sits one eternal cloud of woe,

And

play, at leaft, the two former of thofe characters at Drury-lane with univerfal admiration.—Mrs. Jordan (no
very bad judge) thinks him, as I am told, the beft Mirabel on the ftage.

* See *Retaliation*.

And from her throat a voice fhe heaves
Like winds that moan thro' ruin'd caves;
The trembling ftage fhe paffes o'er,
As if fhe ftepp'd knee deep in gore ;
And every difmal glance fhe fcowls,
Seems caft at daggers, racks, and bowls.
But this is error;—fterneft grief
Bars not the foul from all relief;
And human feelings ne'er remain
Stretch'd on the unceafing rack of pain.—
Poor Shore, fome rays of hope beguile,
And Denmark's queen muft fometimes fmile ;
Maternal joy, in Conftance, fpeaks,
And lives on Lady Randolph's cheeks.—
Short is the beam that breaks the night
Of grief, but thence 'tis doubly bright,
And woe fo touching ne'er appears,
As April fmiles, thro' fhowers of tears.

Could but our fair one, learn to bear
An eafier look, and lighter air,,

Give

Give more emotion to her face,
And to her fhape a *varying* grace;
With fo much feeling, fo much fenfe,
We'd own her claim to eminence—
Confefs her eafily the queen
Of all that fweep *our* tragic fcene,
And fix her * place between, (let's fay)
Siddons and W-lft-in, juft half way.

TO

* On the fubject of the refpective merits of Mrs. G-li-do and Mifs W-lft-in, I can eafily believe, that my adjudication will be difputed by the admirers of the latter, "car la *beauté* eft dangereufe, et il n'y a pas de "venin plus capable de *corrompre l'integrité* d'une juge." But I guefs the public will be, in general, of my opinion.—Mrs. G-li-do is too *lugubre*, but fhe is ftill a very good actrefs *in her line*; and to do her juftice, *fhe* never makes herfelf ridiculous, by attempting parts in which fhe is not, in fome degree, fitted for.

FREDERICK J——S, Esq.

THIRD EPISTLE.

Quoniam femper appetentes gloriæ atque avidi
laudis fuiftis, delenda vobis eft illa macula.

Cic. pro. L. M.

IF youth and lovelinefs could charm,
Or fhape the critic coldnefs warm,
Could gay variety difpenfe
On every effay, excellence ;
And were we only bound to tell
How *much* one plays, and not how *well*;—
To W-lft-in * then, this votive line,
A galaxey of praife fhould fhine,

And

* W-lft-in. On revifing my opinion of this young
lady, I find that it is perhaps too favourable—but
n'imforte, the world always receives a *man's* commenda-
tions of a pretty woman, *cum grano falis.*

And every word I write upon her,
Should offer eulogy and honour ;—
But *she* whom all purfuits engage,
This female proteus of the ftage,
Who thro' all nature boldly flies,
And in one little fortnight tries
Califta, Yarico, and Nell,
And poor Sir Peter's rural belle,
Cannot, in reafon, hope to claim
In *all* her parts, an equal fame.
I own her feeling, tafte and fpirit,
Her verfatility of merit,
I own that it were hard to find
In one, more excellence combin'd ;
But fhould fhe therefore grafp at all,
The gay, the grave, the great, the fmall ;
And, vainly, prove herfelf at heart
A kind of Crow-ftreet Bonaparte ?
Will no one whifper, that fhe plays ill
The froward mirth of Lady Teazle ;

Or

Or hint that nothing can beguile,

To *humour*, her fepulchral * fmile.

Her eye in tragic glances roll'd,

The length'ning nofe of Kemble mould,

And chin eternal, muft prevent

Her looking *archly* innocent.

Young Mirabel † by Kemble play'd,

Look'd like Macbeth in mafquerade—

And

* Sepulchral fmile. A legal wit faid of a brother barrifter, that a fmile on his countenance was like plating on a coffin. Such is Mifs W–lft–in's attempt to look fprightly : She plays the gay parts of Mifs Hardy tolerably, becaufe fhe plays them in a mafk. To her fuccefs, however in this character, we are to attribute a good deal of the vanity I complain of, I wifh fhe could get fome of her *male acquaintance* to tranflate for her ufe, this excellent precept of Horace :

Memento—fervare mentem,

Ab infolenti temperatam

Lætitiâ.

OD. 3. LIB. 2.

† I have had the misfortune to fee this exhibition, truly it was, as Shakefpeare fays, " moft tragical mirth."

And Siddons ‡ in her mirth we find

Mixing up Shore with Rofalind ; §

Learn, W-lft-in from their baffled pride,

To follow *nature* as your guide,

Or—but the candid mufe will fpare

Comparifons 't were hard to bear !—

Alas ! how willingly I'd raife

The fong of undiminifhed praife ;

If, fpite of beauty and of youth,

You were not ftill lefs fair than *truth,* *

D   Believe

‡ Mifs W-lft-in feems to have no more objection to appear in breeches before two or three hundred men, than Mrs. Siddons—tho' they are equal in modefty, they are very unlike in perfonal attractions, and poor Siddons did leaft mifchief.

§ I have heard of a lady who wept plentifully throughout the whole of " As you like it," from an un-happy opinion, that Rofalind was Jane Shore. I am glad to relate the anecdote that fo much good tears fhould not go for nothing.

* Truth. Amicus Plato magis amica veritas.

Believe me W-lft-in that I blame
The fpots of error on your fame,
Only in hopes to fee it rife,
The unclouded radiance of our fkies.

But who is this, all boots and breeches,
Cravat and cape, and fpurs and fwitches,
Grin and grimace and fhrugs and capers,
And affectation, fpleen, and vapours?
Oh, Mr. Richard J———s, * your humble;
Prithee give o'er to mouth and mumble;
Stand ftill, fpeak plain, and let us hear
What was intended for the ear,

For

* Richard J———s. This youth has a kind of merit,
which he greatly overates, but which a little ftudy and
fome flight efforts at remedying the original defects of
education and manners, may improve to perhaps more
than refpectability. He is almoft always lively, never rational, fometimes amufing, feldom intelligible: on a ftage
nearly barren of merit, it is natural he fhould be "*fêté*"
unoculus inter cæcos, is a very confiderable perfon. He
is

For faith without the timely aid,

Of bills, no parts you've ever played,

Handy, Shuffleton, or Rover,

Sharper, Stroller, Lounger, Lover,

Could I amidst your mad-cap pother

Ever distinguish from each other.

Lewis 'tis true that * jumps and prates,

And mutters and extravagates;

D 2 But

is almost the " acteur gâté" that Gil Blas describes, " a qui le parterre pardonne tout; on lui marquoit trop le plaisir que l'on prenoit a le voir, aussi en abusait-il; si l'on eût sifflé; au lieu de crier miracle, on lui auroit *souvent* rendu justice."—Let *me* however do justice to his Diddler; the character is luckily as extravagant (I mean *metaphorically*) as the actor; and both are wonderfully outrés and entertaining.

* Lewis, has great faults and great beauties; why should not R. J——s be as capable of imitating the latter as the former?—He has undoubtedly no inconsiderable disposition towards making a good actor, and I own I should not have treated him so *cavalierly*, but that I perceive him to be nearly spoiled by *over-praise*; my *over fastidiousness* I am not inclined to deny, and so

I should

But then it equally as true is

That Mr. J——s ! you are not Lewis. ‡

    Perennial H—cb—ck now appears,

Victorious o'er the froft of years ;

Fresh flowers adorn her latest days,

A kind of thefpian *aloes.*—

Bleft in each walk of focial life,

Unwrung by care, unvexed by ftrife ;

With placid mind and temperate foul

She fees old Time innoxious roll,

                                    And

I should hope a fair eftimate may be made of his merit. It is juft to add, that he is very correct and very affiduous in his new parts. " Juvat me *hoc* tribuiffe."

‡ Lewis, Pope, and fome others, feeling the abfolute neceffity of fome portion of literature in the compofition of a good player, took very confiderable trouble in this regard, even after they had been fome time on the ftage ; yet neither of them had been a mere mechanic.—Whilft Mr. J——s fhould be ftudying his profeffion, he is to be feen walking up and down Dame-ftreet, canvaffing falutes from every well dreffed man, who will condefcend to nod to him : " Good den, Sir Richard,—Gad a mercy, *fellow.*"

And from his favouring pinions ſhed
Age unoppreſſive o'er her head.

  Her acting not unlike her fate,
Nor meanly low, nor brightly great,
She walks the ſtage's middle courſe
Without or feebleneſs or force ;
And whatſoe'er ſhe act, our eyes
No faults offend, or powers ſurprize.

  But, let me own, that were ſhe bleſſed
With talents, ſuch as Pope * poſſeſſed,
They ſhould not take a greater ſcope,
Or ſtrive to figure more than Pope.

D 3

And

  * Miſs Pope. *Le dernier rejetton* of the old ſchool,
the pupil of the Garricks, the imitator of the Clives,
and the beſt actreſs that the men of our day ever have
ſeen, or perhaps ever will ſee. Thoſe who have had
the happineſs to ſee her Mrs. Heildleberg with King's
Lord Ogleby, and Wewitzer's Canton, in the Clandeſ-
tine Marriage, may form an opinion of " how plays
ſhould be acted."

And we muſt grieve to ſee her play

Every † part and every day,

The young, the old, coquette, or prude,

Poliſhed dame, or houſewife rude—

Till ſurfeited at laſt, we feel

The truth of " la pâté d'anguille." *

Next

† This is by no means the reſult of a *miſ-timed* vanity in Mrs. H—ch—ck; it is the neceſſary conſequence of the miſerable deficiency of good actreſſes, with which our drama is afflicted.—The public is rather under obligations to Mrs. H—ch—ck, for the readineſs with which ſhe undertakes every thing that ſhe thinks can conduce to their entertainment.

The variety of parts ſhe is obliged by the poverty of the company to ſtudy and play, muſt be very diſtreſſing to a perſon of her age and ſituation—

Nil parciunt Seni

Si quæ laborioſa eſt, ad eam curritur

Sin lenis eſt, ad aliam defertur.

TER. prol. in Heautontim.

* Setting out of the queſtion the abſurdity of ſeeing

an

Next W—ll—ms * comes the rude and rough,
With face moſt whimſically gruff,
Aping the carelefs fons of ocean,
He ſcorns each fine and eafy motion ;
Tight to his ſides his elbows pins,
And dabbles with his hands like fins ;
Would he diſplay the greateſt woe,
He flaps his breaſt, and points his toe ;

Is

an old woman (whatever be her vigor and talents)
playing girliſh parts, I muſt confefs that in theatrical
matters " *diverſité* (not *novelty*" take notice) *eſt ma deviſe.*" La Fontaine, La Pâté d'anguille.

* W—ll—ms. This man plays fecond-rate characters, with fourth-rate abilities—Some of his failors are
very well ; and of this he is fo fatisfied, that knowing
where his talent lies, he turns *all* his parts into *failors.*
His Crabtree, his Job Thornberry, his Ibrahim, are difmal inſtances of this *amphibious* merit.

Is merriment to be expreffed,
He points his toe and flaps his breaft.
His turns are fwings,—his ftep a jump,
His feelings fits,—his touch a thump;
And violent in all his parts,
He fpeaks by gufts, and moves by ftarts.

   And lo! his wife, whofe every feature
Foretells the talent of the creature;
Lively and vulgar, low and pert
She plays, *au vif*, the peafant flirt,
And hits, without the flighteft aid
From *Art*, the faucy chamber-maid. *

Oh!

   * Format enim *natura* prius nos *intus* ad omnem
Fortunarum habitum—
   I am fure nature never intended Mrs. W—ll—ms for
a fine lady, or even for a fine gentleman, a character fhe
fometimes attempts. It is really difgraceful, that there
fhould be no actrefs on the Dublin ftage, capable of playing the well bred female characters of our beft plays;
poor Mrs. W—ll—ms is obliged to give up a line of
acting in which fhe is very refpectable, to ftop by
the

Oh! could a little fenfe controul

The flights of her afpiring foul ;—

Could fhe be fatisfied with all

The glories of the fervants'-hall,

Nor e'er with daring fteps prefume

To figure in the drawing room ;—

Could fhe but wifely be content

With *Mincing* and not *Millamant*,

And following nature's humble courfe,

Decline *Bifarre* and play *Lamorce*,

None would have gueffed that fhe had ne'er

Obferved what life and manners were,

Nor

the moft ridiculous efforts, the gaps of the company—this is a heavy misfortune to the audience, but, " en revanche," 'tis a great faving to the managers—good ac-treffes demand good falaries, and Mrs. W—ll—ms is fo much clear gain—

> " Intercà *guftus* elementa per omnia quærunt
> " Nunquam animo *pretiis obftantibus*"

Oh! guftus and actreffes are very different things to a man of *tafte*.—

Nor ever known a circle higher
Than that around the green-room fire.

  'Tis shame to offer to the view,
This kind of " *payfanne parvenue*"
This Nell in lady's robes arrayed,
This *hafh* of miftrefs and of maid.
And yet not all the blame attaches
To her,—fhe naturally fnatches,
At fpangled gowns, and caps of lace,
To mend her figure and her face—
But why this travefty permitted ?
Becaufe we've no one better fitted ;
And thus in utter difregard
Of right or wrong, our plays are marred ;
An ufeful actrefs is difgraced,
And infult braves the public tafte.

FOURTH

FOURTH EPISTLE.

————————tragœdus
Sub nutrice, velut fi *luderet infans.*

Hor. Epis. ad Aug

Hush! 'tis attention all around.
Fixed is each eye and ftilled each found,
Silence on every lip is preffed,
And pleafure throbs in every breaft.
What is to come? will Barry rife,
Or Garrick glad our wond'ring eyes?
What miracle is to be wrought
Beyond the common fcope of thought?
" The cry is now they come, they come"
And lo! Glenalvon, and—Tom Thumb : *

Now

* A child of the name of Beatty, a native of Belfaft,
has been very lately added to the force of the company,
" mercy on us, a bearne ; a very pretty bearne" indeed
—but fo young, as even in the part of Douglas, to throw

an

Now clapping hands, and loud huzzas
Thunder the rapture of applaufe,
The very walls are rocked and why—
The hero's only *four* feet high!
The noife redoubles,—we are told
The hero's only *twelve* years old!
But oh! what language could we find,
The raptures of the critic mind
To tell, could we our Douglafs * call,
But *two years* old, and *two feet* tall!!!

No

an appearance of ridicule and fantocinity over the whole
performance.   This folly of exhibiting children, is not
quite modern.   " There is, Sir," fays Rofincrantz to
Hamlet " an *airy* of *young children, little eyafes,* that
cry out on the top of queftion, and are moft tyrannical-
ly *clapped* for it.—Thefe are now the fafhion"—but I believe it never was, before this year, the fafhion to introduce *one* infant to play the firft charaéters among men
and women—oh! 'tis a dainty device to attraét an audience, Daly's poney races were not much worfe.

* Douglas.   Though I only take notice of this part,
it is meet to fet it down, that the infant played Romeo

to

No wonder Randolph fhould be jealous,
He fuch a charming little fellow 's,
See how he fteps in ftately pride
At leaft fix inches every ftride,
See how he fwells with lordly rage
Altho' no higher than a page ;—
In vain two barons † ftout and gaunt,
The little Grildrig ftrive to daunt,
O'er both he triumphs, and alack!
Slays one ;—*Oh giant-killing Jack!!!*

And is this then the won'drous bait
For loud applaufe and houfes great,

E

The

to Mrs. Kni—ton's Juliet, and that they looked like an overgrown girl and her doll. I fhould not be much amazed to fee him advertifed for Henry the VIII. or Sir John Falftaffe.—He has alfo played Prince Arthur: this was as it fhould be, mirabile dictu!—

† The victory of Beatty over Hargrave, (Infelix puer atque; impar congreffus Achilli) was like the battles in Mother Goofe's tales, in which fairies never fail to overcome giants; but the wonder is not greater than that one individual fhould fubdue the good fenfe of a whole city, into thraldom.

The Roſcius, * this, whoſe radiance bright,
Should dim the ineffectual light
Of all the glow-worms of the ſtage,
Of every ſize and every age ?—

An infant † taken from his ſchool,
A pitying public to befool,

A baby

* Roſcius.   This was the *modeſt* title under which
the " little eyaſe," was announced " ad captandum
vulgus," and it did its office with a vengeance.   I heard
ſome of my brethren of the pit diſcourſing, " who this
Roſcius could be;" one learned gentleman aſſerted, that
it was one Garrick's chriſtian name ; but the general
opinion ſeemed to be, that he was a French actor, who
had been guillotined in the early days of the revolution.
Thoſe critics I obſerved to be particularly loud and *judicious* in their applauſes, as might be ſuppoſed.

† Children have ever been an engine of pity and
pardon;

—————— Speak, thou *boy*,
Perhaps thy *childiſhneſs* will move them more
Than our reaſon—

but in this inſtance the very production of the intercef-
for is an aggravation.

A baby victim, to atone
For all the faults of folks full grown :
As for the people's sins, of old
They flew the firstling of the fold,
And thought the *Gods* could never damn
Those who should sacrifice a lamb.

Poor child, thy age and infant fears,
Thy * talents far beyond thy years,
Thy simple tones untuned by art,
Would melt to praise the critic heart,
Were praise not ruin;—if you now
To plain advice refuse to bow,

E 2   And

* La quale (difpofitione) accompagnata dal' ajuto ordinario delle forze umane, può un giorno, rendere *quel giovine* de fommo talento. Vir. de Sifto. V.

I do not deny the *boy's* abilities, but I protest against turning the stage into a nursery ; and I lament that a promising child should be deprived " del' ajuto ordinario," which might make him an useful man, to be converted into a source of theatrical revenue, and public ridicule.—" Young men," says Bacon, " should be *learners*, while men grown up are *actors* :"—This is true in every sense.

And rather lay thy boyiſh claim
To guſts of praiſe, than laſting fame ;—
For ſome few months we'll call you clever,
And then,—poor child,—farewell for ever."
But to thy ſtudies hence again—
Turn the page, and guide the pen ;
Leave to the fribble † and the fool,
To ſcorn the ſeaſoning of the ſchool.
In Hiſtory's magic glaſs, deſcry
How ſages live, and heroes die,

From

† The number of good actors who were not men of
education is very ſmall : but now a days we imagine
that all talents come by inſpiration, and that great abilities are the reſult of the temporary exertion of what are
called, our *energies.*—" Tout eſt bien, ſortant des mains
de l'auteur des choſes, tout dégénère entre les mains
de l'homme." Many perſons ſeem to have read no farther in Emile than the firſt ſentence, which is the moſt
falſe and ſophiſtical in the whole work—*et c'eſt beaucoup dire.*

From lively Greece,‡ and fober Rome,

Import their manners and coftume, †

Weigh all thy parts with learned care,

Be firft a critic, then a player ;—

And when, too foon, the flight of time

Shall give thy fhape its manly prime,

And thought, and ftudy have refin'd,

And ftored with claffic tafte thy mind ;

E 3

Then

‡ Fatendum Latinos fere à Græcis vinci *lepôre*, fed vincere *gravitate*. Voss. de Poet. Lat. c. 7.

† Were it not for fome men of education who, luckily for the pleafures of the world, became managers and actors, we fhould ftill have Cato played in a full-bottomed wig, and Coriolanus en habit galonné, and perugue a la reine—

When from the court a birth-day fuit beftowed,
Sinks the laft actor in a tawdry load.
Booth enters ;—hark ! the univerfal peal !
" But has he fpoken ?"—not a fyllable,
" What fhook the ftage and made the people ftare?"
Cato's long *wig, flower'd* gown, and lacquer'd chair.

POPE.

" Il portait," fays Scarron of M. Le Deftin, des *chauffes trouffées* a bas d'attache comme celles des comediens quand ils reprèfentent un *héros de l'antiquité.*"

Then to the fcene return, and claim
Thy well-learned mead,—perennial fame. §

 Enough;—fair Kn—ton * now to you——
The poet's critic fong is due;
Mild and attractive—nature's mould
Ne'er formed thee for the loud and bold—
To rule with haughty Margaret's air,
To fhriek Alicia's mad defpair,

To

§ I have given, perhaps, to Beatty more than his
fhare of attention, but I fhall not lament my trouble,
if I fhould have any influence in diffuading him from
perfifting *at prefent*, in his dramatic purfuits, and in
reftoring him to the leffons of his mafters 'till he can
fay with the fon of Ulyffes :—

 —— ἐγω δ' ἐτι νήπιος ἦα.
Νῦν δ'ὅτε δη μέγας εἰμι, κ) αλλων μυθον ἀκυων
Πυνθάνομαι, κ) δη μοι ἀέξεται ἐνδοθι θυμὸς,
Πειρήσω.——

* Kn—ton. This lady has fome neglected capabi-
lities about her, but fhe is one of the moft inanimate
actreffes I have ever feen.

To pour with Conftance, hatred's flood,
Or grafp the daggers fteeped in blood.
It *meant* thee for the gentler parts
Of moiftened eyes, and melting hearts;
The humble † fympathetic friend,
Prompt to weep—to bear—to bend,
The duteous child, fubmiffive wife,
And all the fofter fhades of life.
But fad reverfe—the face and form
Which *art* might animate and warm,
You clearly fhew in every part,
Have never known the care of art.
And thus the choiceft gifts are loft,
‡ Torpor your calm,—your mildnefs froft;

Untouched

† In *heroic foubrettes*, the Annas, the Cleones, and the Cephifas, Mrs. Kn—ton might be very refpectable. We could wifh to fee her name fubftituted in general, for that of Mrs. Chal—ers, who is by no means fit *even* for the parts fhe plays.

‡ It is very agreeable to me to be able to fay, that in fome paffages of the character of Amelrofa, Mrs. Kn—ton was an exception to herfelf—fhe was animated and affecting.

Untouched you fmile,—unmoved you weep,—
Your voice a dream—your filence fleep.

To bear our opera's whole weight,
The atlas of our vocal ftate,
Who of all Crow-ftreet's fons alone,
Can read a note or fwell a tone,
Comes fmirking Phi—ips* full of graces,
Tottering in his girlifh paces,
With feeble voice, yet fweet and true,
(Where tafte has done, what tafte can do.)

But

* Phi—ips has fome merit as a finger;—His voice is
however, better adapted to a room, than to a theatre—
and to the accompaniment of a forte-piano, than of an
orcheftra—but he is, as I am informed, fo into-
lerably vain, that it is fometimes difficult to induce him
to play. Singers have ever been remarked for their
capricioufnefs, but even he whom Horace ridicules for
that folly, did not as would feem, prefume to carry it
farther than his own private circle.

" Omnibus hoc vitium eft cantoribus, *inter amicos*
" Ut nunquam inducant animum cantare rogati."

Tigellius would never, I dare fwear, difappoint the *public*.

But of his pipe fo vain withal,
That faith he never fings at all—
Poor gentleman, he's moved with wonder,
That folks fhould think *he*'d act Leander— *
But if you give the parts of Braham,
Perhaps he'll condefcend to play 'em;
Or if you beg it, will attack a
Bravura, Arriette, Polacca,
But to fing every common air,
Is more than gentlemen † can bear.

Be

* Mr. Phi—ips is reported to have refufed the part of Leander in the Padlock, as below his mark; and ftill more wonderful to relate, they had no one to fupply his place, Mr. Phi—ips being the only profeffed finger at prefent on the Irifh ftage, except Meffrs. Co—e and Li—fay, who, I fuppofe, declined the character alfo. I fhould have been much pleafed to have feen either of thofe latter gentlemen attempt it, "it would be argument for a week, laughter for a month, and a good jeft for ever."

† Mr. Phi—ips, I am told, piques himfelf on being much of a gentleman, I am exceedingly glad of it; and

as

Be not, good Sir, fo wond'rous vain,
Tho' heaven beftowed the vocal ftrain——
All but yourfelf can fee, you're curfed
To fing the beft and act the worft. *

FIFTH

as it is now become quite *vulgar* to be indifpofed, we
hope he will get entirely well of thofe *fudden* and *periodic colds* that fo often affect him, and deprive us of
the pleafure of hearing him. Is Mr. Phi——ips afhamed
of a title which the firft Lord of the Treafury boafts of,
that of a *fervant* of the public?

    * At prefent I fhall fay no more of this mufcadin-
fongfter——but

        Habeo alia multa quæ nunc condonabitur.
        Quæ proferentur poft, *fi perget* tædere.
                                        TER.

FIFTH EPISTLE.

Tota armenta fequuntur.

ALN. L. I

" WHAT? ecce interum Crifpinus"

" I'm gone"—nay, Fred'rick, don't refign us,

Nor like a coward fneak away

Juft in the middle of the fray.

Take patience, man, refume your courage

And fight it out without demurrage—

Think what a fubject of contention,

Should we ev'n *one* forget to mention

" 'Twere better" hark their general call

" Be damned, than noticed not at all,"

Befides 'tis but a *debt* you pay,

For I have oft fat out the play.

And

And borne without complaints or grudges
Your Archers, * Tancreds, Falconbridges,
Nor fuffered hifs t' efcape my tongue,
Tho' Ph—ips played, and Li—fay fung ;
And fure, however hard to bear,
My verfes can't be worfe than they are.

   Come then ! lead on the rear-guard, F-ll-m, *
Who with deputed truncheon rule 'em ;
And tho' the buffo of the band,
Tower the fecond in command.

                           (Thus

   * Archers, Tancred's, Falconbridges. Who ever
has fat out the plays, in which thefe characters are, as
they have been lately reprefented, have indeed more
than common claims on the Patentee's gratitude. Richard J——s in Archer, was the leaft exceptionable of the
triad and the infant, the moft contemptible. Heu mife-
rande Puer!

   * F-ll-m is the acting manager, and we are not therefore to be furprifed at finding his own characters in the
front of every bill; it is natural, and I fhould be well
content, but that with an unhappy, tho' not uncommon
                          fatality,

(Thus as old * comedies record,
Chriftophero Sly, became a lord,)—

Cheer up! nor look fo plaguy four,
I own your merit, feel your power.
And from my prudent lips fhall flow,
Words † as light as flakes of fnow :
For fhould I vex you, well you might
Repay 't, by playing every night ;
And furnifhed with moft potent engines,
Gubbins or *Scrub*,—take ample vengeance.

But truce with gibing, let's be fair—
Fullam's a very pleafant player ;
In knavifh craft, and tefty age, ‡
Sly mirth, and impotence of rage;

F

He's

fatality, his favourite parts are thofe which he plays
worft ;—His Scrub is execrable, and his Gubbins very
indifferent.

* Induction to the Taming of a Shrew.

† ἔπεα νιφάδεσσιν ἐοικότα χειμερίῃσιν.   IL. 3.

‡ Vivaces agit violentus iras.

SENEC. H. F.

He's ftill, tho' often harfh and mean,
The eveneft actor of our fcene.

Hargrave * the modeft and the meek,
With humble blufhes clothes his cheek;
Seems fcarcely bold enough to raife
His eyes, indifferent of praife,
And with demeanour mildly proud,
Retires in filence from the crowd.
To him indeed, one vainly looks
For Kemble's rival, or for Cooke's,
Yet oft he glads the critic eyes
With gleams from talent's pureft fkies;
And draws the tear, and melts the heart
By carelefs ftrokes of happieft art:

Oh!

* I was much perplexed in forming an opinion of
Mr Hargrave's dramatic merit, as he is really one of
the moft uneven actors I ever faw. Had his *private*
character been the fubject of confideration, I fhould
not

Oh! fi fic omnia,—but alas!

Thofe gleams like winter's funfhine pafs.

He feems to think a fmiling face

And upright pofture a difgrace,

And therefore labours to prefent

His vifage crofs, his body bent—

As if his fenfe perceived around,

Unfavoury fmell, or difmal found.

And thus we're left to wonder ftill

Who plays fo well, fhould play fo ill.

What fair ones next advance in rank,

Davis † plump, and Stuart lank—

O'er Davis, let us draw the veil,

Nor touch, e'er wounds have time to heal.

F 2   Let,

not have hefitated a moment, to fay that it is one of the
moft refpectable I have heard of.

* **Davis.** I had much to fay of this lady, but at this
moment praife would be loft to her, and cenfure would
be cruel.

Let, undisturbed by satire, flow
The sacred stream of private woe,
Nor mortal hand to touch presume
The widow, weeping o'er the tomb.

Poor Stuart * too, has claims for grace;
Inveterate wedlock in her face,
Pleads with more eloquence for pity
Than all the preachers of the city :
Poor girl! *sufficient* torments teize you,
I will not blame, and cannot praise you.

What

* This little woman, under the name of Miss Grif-
fiths, played for some time with confiderable applaufe,
for which fhe was indebted principally to a lively manner, and a pretty fhape—

Sed longum *forma* percurrens iter
Deperdit aliquid femper, et fulget minus
Nec *illa Venus* eft.

HER. OET.

Her beauty (if it can be fo called) is common to our
eyes, and worn fo threadbare, that it no longer covers
her multitude of fins: and her livelinefs fhe has com-
pletely

What dreadful founds affail my ear,
Are all the coffin-makers here ?
Do creaking cars bear grumbling fwine?
Does grating F——t * fright the nine ?
C—ke † play eight inftruments together,
Or croaking frogs foretell wet weather ?

F 3   Or

pletely loft with her ' pucellage'—far be it from me,
to guefs whence the alteration proceeds ; but it is vifible
and really afflicting.   *Omne animal*— 'the proverb is
fomewhat mufty'.—

She was a tolerable Ariel, and was admired in fome
other light characters—but at this moment fhe is f.t for
nothing, but bearing Juliet's or Ophelia's pall.

* For this gentleman's appearance on this ftage, he
has to thank his own and Mr. T. C—ke's indifcretion—
they will underftand me—if they fhould not, Mr.
G-li-do may affift their memories.

† The *never*-fufficiently-to-be-extolled leader of the
band, whom I have fo often mentioned — it occurs to me,
that he *committed* the *diffonance* alluded to ; that, from
doing fo much in *ore* evening, he might have leave ever
after to retire at the end of the fourth act of the play, and
abandon

Or is it Li—fay's * Irifh howl?

Or folemn C-yne's pedantic growl?

'Tis both—in difmal chaunt they join,

And Li—fay's echoed back by C-yne.

So

abandon the ballet and farces to the guidance of his un-
derlings.—Meffrs. *Salomon*, *Weifchel*, *Cramer*, or *Shaw*,
who are, in fome degree Mr. C—ke's *equals*, never prefumed to take fuch liberty; and I beg Mr. C—ke will
confider whether it is decorous or refpectful to the public or his employer.

* Li—fay. This perfon is the *only* actor of Irifh
characters, now on the Irifh ftage, and the laft w e had
was a *Welchman*. This is one of our practical bulls.—
Li—fay is however not only the Denis Brulgruddery,
and the Sir Lucius O'Trigger of Dublin, but is alfo,
poor man! one of our principal vocal performers. M r.
C-yne enacts the dignified and elegant Sir Philip Blandford, and the plain Steadfaft, and even fometimes the
mad Octavian; but he nevertheless condefcends to of-
ficiate " invito Apollone" as one of the *tuneful train*.
To both thofe gentlemen, we may, without exaggera-
tion, apply the ancient epigram

Νυκτικοραξ αδει θανατηφορον· αλλ' οταν αση
Δημ φιλος, θνσκει κ' αυτος νυκτικοραξ.

Ανθολ. Δευτ. **XXV.**

So at the morning's early hours,
One jack-afs tries his tuneful powers;
And quick another's difmal throat
Brays dreadful a refponfive note,
It roars thro' cow-houfe, barn and fty,
Horfeponds and ditches loud reply;
The pigs affrighted fcamper wild,
And * the vexed mother whips her child.

  Good folks, I owe you no ill will;
Be Blandford, or O'Trigger ftill,
Act as you like, or right or wrong,
But ne'er again attempt a *fong*.

And

   * Et trepidæ matres preffere ad pectora natos.

A<small>N</small>. 7.

  In Ireland, the cuftom in cafes of vexation and terror, is different from that of the Romans, as thofe who
know any thing of the Irifh cottager's manners can tef-
tify. I hope I have however preferved the *fpirit* of the
famous paffage I allude to.

And now comes every namelefs name, ✳

The public torture and the fhame,

Who nightly as the curtains rife

Offend our ears and fcare our eyes ;

Kings, footmen, fenators and hags

In ermine, livery, or rags.

Thick in terrific groups, they mix

Like ghofts upon the banks of Styx ; †

But

✳ One perfon however, not named in the laft, I muft diftinguifh from this general judgment.—Mr. Waylett— of whom I have feen too little to be able to applaud him, and too much to pafs him over in utter filence. He played Sir Oliver Surface one night, with a plain fimplicity and eafe, that made a very favourable impreffion—I hope it may not be defaced.

† Huc omnis turba ad ripas effufa ruebat,
Matres atq ; viri, *defunctaq* ; *corpora vitâ*
Magnanimûm heroum, *pueri*, innuptæq ; *puellæ.*

Aen. 6.

The refemblance lies, not in their numbers or appearances alone, but, in the " defuncta corpora vitâ" alfo.

But fo felf-fatisfied, 'tis plain
That they inflict, not fuffer pain :
Low and conceited, pert and dull,
Each empty brain, and leaden fcull,
Each crofs-made fhape, and gorgon face
Lay claims to beauty, fenfe, and grace ;—
Claims let them make—th' indignant mufe
Stoops not t' admit them, or refufe ;
She gives them neither praife or blame *
And to the *moon* † configns each name
(Where connoiffeurs collections fhow
Of all that's loft on earth below,)
There in dark cafes let them fit
With O's ‡ fkill, and V's wit;

D's

    * ——— Quefto mifero modo
  Téngon l'anime trifte di coloro
  Che viffer fanza infamia e fanza lodo.
                    DANT. Infern. C. 3.

† Vide ORL. FURIOS.

‡ Whether thefe letters be initial or final, whether
                                                    they

D's virture,—A's youth,

S's good temper,—D's truth,

P's pity,—M's pence,

R's time,—and T's fenfe.

SIXTH

they fignify names, or indeed whether they mean any thing at all, I muft be excufed from difclofing.

If they have no fignification, why fhould I betray my own nonfenfe? and if they be typical, it belongs to the public to make the application.

SIXTH EPISTLE.

Εγὼ μὲν δὴ οἶμαι ἅπερ υπεθέμην ἀπειργάσθαι—ἰι δέ
τις ταναντία ἐμοὶ γιΓνώςκει τὰ ἔργα αυτων επισκοπῶν,
εὑρήσει αὐ͵α μαρτυρͤντα, τοῖς εμοῖς λόγοις.

XENOPH. Cyr. Lib. VIII.

Good natured mufe that from the fky
Breathe on encomiaftic Pye,
And deck his periodic lays
With honied trope and flowery phrafe;
Deign on your fuppliant bard to fhower
The gentleft influence of your power,
And teach my voice to celebrate
The glories of the thefpian ftate;

'Tis

* 'Tis my laſt work—my laſt requeſt,
This labour o'er, from verſe I reſt—
Beſides my lays to J——s belong,
What muſe to J——s denies a ſong.

  She hears me not—in vain I pray,
Fair Eulogy is far away,
Teaching young preachers to diſcloſe
The beauties of poetic proſe,
And guiding laureate bards to try
Flights of proſaic poetry.

  But lo! uncalled, from routs and drums
Dame Cenſure to my cloſet comes ;
Of Journals floats her patchwork gown,
Poſt, Courier, Chronicle and Sun,
And, to ſupply the 'kerchief's ends,
A *Cobbett* from her ſides depends;
Inſtead of *attar*, round her head
Steams of *tea* their incenſe ſhed—

Her

---

  * Extremum hunc Arethuſa mihi concede laborem,
    Pauca meo Gallo——————
      —————— neget quis carmina Gallo. Virg. Ecl. X·

Her ears two figured serpents deck,
And beads of *black-beans* twine her neck,
Wreathed o'er her forehead nettles nod,
In place of *fan*, a wormwood rod
She bears ; and hanging from her breast
Churchill in miniature expressed.

" Write on" she cries, " obey my power;
" These are my subjects, this my hour :
" Thalia and Melpomene
" Their kingdoms abdicate to me,
" And all distinctions I o'erwhelm
" By *union* * of my double realm.—
" Of yore there was a bound between
" The tragic and the comic scene.

G   " Smirking

* Since the days of the universal Garrick, every
stroller thinks he can play every thing ; tragedy, comedy, farce, and pantomime.—Actors seem now to think
it quite disgraceful to be excellent in one line alone

" The mouse that is content with one poor hole,
" Can never be a mouse of any soul."

" Smirking features—tripping gait

" Ne'er troubled the feverer ſtate ;

" Nor hollow voice, nor formal ſtalk

" E'er treſpaſſed on the comic walk,

" Each kept its humour and its place,

" Peculiar gait, and natural face.

" But now confounded, melted, mixed,

" No frontier barrier betwixt

" Our actors different changes try

" The † tragic grin, the comic cry.

" Each face ſo ſevered into halves,

" That one ſide weeps while t' other laughs :

" Thus

† In this reſpect the audience frequently imitates hem—I have ſeldom ſeen more merry faces, than at a German tragedy—a German tragedy, is a kind of " Tragedy for warm weather," and a German comedy alſo approaches ſo nearly to the ſtandard of that celebrated piece, that there is no longer any diſtinction between the ſpecies of the drama : to the modern we may apply what Tacitus ſays of the ancient Germans " Genus ſpectaculorum *unum* et in *omni cœtu idem.*"

" Thus Irish weddings oft display

" Mixed scenes of frolick and of fray ;

" And at their funerals and wakes

" Close by the coffin laughter shakes.

" Or thus in prints, you think you've got

" The features of a jolly fot :

" But look again, and you behold

" The furious visage of a scold.

    " Though these my subjects are unfit

" For Otway's pathos, Congreve's wit,

" They in such dramas hope to tower,

" As suit their heteroclite power.

" —In *tragedies* * that offer ranting

" For spirit, and for pathos canting,

G 2   " Blustering

* "Audiences are now drawn together by the translated trash of some foreign novelty,—they wait the appearance of a ghost or a goblin ; they hope to be roused from their weary lethargy, into hysterical laughter, or hysterical tears, by the *farcical* or the *horrid*—they swallow with gaping wonder, the eccentric flights, the profane rants, the illuminated morality, the bombastic diction

of

" Bluftering for forrow, oaths for fighs,

" For vigour, rage and blafphemies :

" Where paffions either creep or fly,

" Meanly low, or madly high,

" And *bedlam-nature* ftalks * or flutters

" Either on ftilts or in the gutters,—

" —In

of imported patchwork from their German favourites."
Prefton's Refiec. on the Germ. Style, p. 59. Every one
who is acquainted with German literature, well knows
that not one of their dramas (*Germania quos horrida par-
turit Fœtus*) deferves to be excepted from this general
cenfure. The Englifh reader I refer to *all* the plays of
Schiller and Kotzebue, which have been tranflated into
our language. He will not find one piece undifgraced
by vice or folly : fome indeed excel in folly, others in
vice, but in general " they are as like one another as
half-pence, each feeming monftrous 'till its fellow come
to match it." As you like it.

* What would Longinus have thought of fuch paffion
and fublimity, as the following paffages (taken at ran-
dom from Schiller) exhibit.

" Now let the ftorm rage, tho' it fhould fwell me up
to the throat" Robbers.

" O. Moor,

" —In *comedies* where pun and hit

" But ill fupply the want of wit,

" And all the incident confifts

" In active * heels, and brawny fifts ;

G 3   " Where

" *O. Moor*. I am no fpirit—but living as thou art—
" oh! life of wretchednefs.

" *Y. Moor*. What, waft thou not buried ?

" *O. Moor*. That is, a dead hound lies in the grave
" of my father." ROBBERS.

" What, talk you of nobility in Genoa? *(indignantly)*
" let them all throw their anceftry and honors into the
" fcale, and one hair from the white beard of my old
" uncle, fhall make it kick the beam." FIISCO.
SCHILLER.

Of thefe effufions, for the faithful tranflation of the two
firft of which I am accountable, Longinus would fay, as
he does of thofe of the *water-feet* of his day, ποιητα
τινος τω οντι εχι νηφοντος ετι. Sec. XXXII. or he
would have referred them βαχχεια τινι των λογων.
to a certain drunkennefs of expreffion, which was fometimes objected to Plato.

* " The public appetite began to be fated with non-
" fenfe, which now required to be reinforced with
                  " practical

" Where polifhed heroes nothing fay

" But * " *zounds keep moving, what 's to pay*"

" And for his plot the author trufts

" To mending † coats, and breaking bufts.—

" —In *operas* ‡ where lovers come

" To dulcet found of bafs § and drum,

" And

" practical jokes, and corporal activity." PRESTON'S
Reflec. p. 65.

* Thefe are fpecimens of the phrafeology of our new
comic fchool, taken from " *a Cure for the Heart-ache,*"
and fome other farrago of folly, of which I, happily,
forget every thing but the cant word that I have quoted.

† On the important incidents of a tailor's mending
his own coat, and a fharper breaking a cracked china
figure, two modern pieces entirely turn.

‡ Here let me fay a word or two on the ftate of our
' corps d'opera' *(opera inanis !)* The *three* female
fingers, Miffes Howells and Davidfon, and Mrs. Stewart, are on every account incapable of playing even
fecondary parts, and indeed feem to me to be only fit
to

" And damfels thrill their tender lay to

" Trombone and trumpet obligato,

" Where harmony's accordant choir

" Is loft in crafh of wood and wire,

" And

to lengthen the proceffion in Alphonfo, or fwell the chorufes of the Caftle Spectre. We have no profeffed male finger but Mr. Phillips, and thus the *whole* of our mufical department depends on his flender pipe. Now as it happens that, from fome caufe or other, this gentleman cannot conveniently play all the parts, both male and female, of an opera on one night, it is evident that it were unreafonable to expect any mufical entertainment at the Dublin theatre. But that we fhould not have to complain of a *tetal* want of this fpecies of amufement, recourfe has been had to a moft brilliant expedient, which for its fingular ingenuity, I fhall relate in detail. Some one had heard that a diftreffed country company, had once played Hamlet with the omiffion of Hamlet's character, and it therefore occurred to them, that a *mufical* entertainment, with the *mufic omitted*, would be in the prefent pofture of affairs, the moft fatisfactory extrication which could be devifed.—The fcheme was, it feems, adopted, and the Battle of Hexham had the honor to be felected for the experiment. The aforefaid
Miffes

" And he o'er all his peers is proudeft,

" Who roars the longeft and the loudeft."

" Thus 'fpite of all their boafted nine,

" The modern theatre is mine;

" There

Miffes H. and D. were to fing all the chorufes, and Mr. Phillips's name appeared in the front of the bills as principal in the glees. Night after night did Mr. Phillips's non-appearance difappoint the weary audiences, 'till at laft Meffrs. Jeffery and Dyke, who ufually enact waiters, fenators, and fuch folk, kindly confented to make themfelves ridiculous, by finging the firft and bafs parts in fuch time and tune, as it fhould pleafe God. So far all was profperous. But here another *unforefeen* accident occurred, for it was by fome means or other difcovered, that the *firft* and *third* would be ufelefs without a *fecond*. Neceffity, fays the proverb, is the mother of invention, and neceffity took a violoncello-teacher, (who is I fancy not at all connected with the theatre, except thro' his brother) dreffed him in a fine brown jerkin, equipped him by the affiftance of a burned cork with moft terrific mouftachios, and finally turned him out upon the ftage a finifhed *fecond*, in whom nothing was forgotten or omitted, but a *voice* to fing—and after

" There every night fupreme I fit

" O'er boxes, gallery, and pit :

" There in my fetters, kingly J——s

" Utters his unavaling groans,

                                    " Long

ter *this manner* the *mufical* drama of the Battle of Hexham was faid and fung by his Majefty's fervants!!! " ex
uno difce omnes."

§ Paufanias in his account of the Cadmean family,
(B.eot. c. 5.) fays, that *Harmony* was the daughter of
Mars and *Venus*. Could I fufpeft any of our compo-
fers of being, '*litterulis græcis imbutus*' I fhould guefs
that, from this paffage, he derived the elegant notion of
accompanying love-fongs with horns, triangles, kettle-
drums, and other martial inftruments—fo that now-a-
days,

 De nos orcheftres, l'harmonie
  N'eft que du bruit et du fracas
 Pour peindre la mélancholie
  Oh offre le bruit des combats
 Pour peindre la paix, l'innocence,
  On prend trombonnes et clarions
 Pour accompagner la romance
  Bientot on prendra du *canon*!!!—
     MARANT.

" Long shall he groan, nor hope to gain

" His suffering kingdoms from my reign,

" 'Till, in his party he can boast

" A brave unmutilated host—

" 'Till Hamlet lead his danish force,

" And English Richard take to horse—

" 'Till Dunsinane send forth its lord,

" And Martius wave his Roman sword—

" 'Till to his aid the tragic band

" Of every time, from every land,

" On German nonsense turn the war,

" And chain down conquest to his car."

    " In vain shall he expect to ride

" In safety o'er the public tide,

" To buffet every gale that blows,

" And sweep the sea of all his foes.

" While in his puny fleet * are reckoned

" First-rates none, but one o' th' second, †

                                 " And

    * The following specimen of a theatrical Lloyd's
List, will give a tolerable recapitulation of my opinions
of the Crow-street company.

                                    Meer's

" And all the reft—his bold defenders

" Are frigates, luggers, hulks, and tenders."

" For

Moor's-head, Jan. 23, 1804.

" Admiral Jones in fpite of the very hard weather
" ftill continues to keep his ftation off the Bagnio-flip.
" If the Peter-ftreet fquadron fhould attempt to put
" to fea, we are confident the gallant Admiral will give
" a good account of them. His force is as follows :"

Ships.	Guns.	Commanders.
Montague	74	Talbot
Veteran	50	Hitchcock (Mrs.)
Charon	44	Vice Ad. Fullam
Affurance	44	R. Jones
Gorgon	44	Galindo (Mrs.)
L'Entreprenante	44	Walftein
Le Modefte	38	Hargrave
Alligator	36	Williams
Tartar	32	Williams (Mrs.)
Fairy	16	Stewart (Mrs.)
Bittern	16	Lindfay
Borer	12	Coyne

" Remains *in port*, La Mufette (en flûte) Phillips."

" We are forry to obferve that the Favourite—Cref-
" well

" For my part, (metaphor afide)

" His weaknefs is my ftrength and pride,

" I die if he plucks up a fpirit,

" For Cenfure lives on want of merit."

She faid and vanifhed,—thro' my room
Vapours arofe of acrid fume.—
Thus when a ghoft his miffion ends,
And thro' the yawning trap defcends,
The yawning trap in clouds expires,
Sulphureous fmell of brimftone fires.

Dear J——s I'm glad the beldame's fled,
Reft fhe for ever with the dead ;
Ne'er may her features, four and cramp,
* Vifit the glimpfes of our lamp,

Making

" well—and the Infolent—Stewart, have *parted company*
" in the late *breezes*"—

Tantâ mole *viri* turritis *puppibus* inftant ! !!

† If the foregoing fcale be correct, he has none either of the firft or fecond-rates, and but one of the
third.

* Revifit'ft thus the glimpfes of the moon
Making night hideous. HAMLET.

Making night hideous ; ne'er again
With bitter taunt and cynic mein,
May fhe invade the facred bound
That fences bard and players round ;
But let us lay this worfe than ghoft,
And fend her to the red-fea coaft
In the due forms of magic fchool,
And exorcife the fiend by rule.

† Firft let us grafp with daring hand
Th' Avonian talifmanic wand,
And fummon here on their allegiance
The powers that pay to it obedience ;—
* Hecate dark, and ‡ Ariel light,
And merry § Robin fportive fprite ;

H Titania,

† The learned reader will perceive fome incongru-
ities in this exorcifm, *que je me garderai bien d'an-
noncer aux ignorans.*

* Macbeth. ‡ Tempeft.

§ Robin Goodfellow. Midfum. Night's Dream.

* Titania, Oberon and all
That hear the fairy monarch's call,
Theirs be the region of the airs,
And conftant watch etherial, theirs.

† Then comes the minifterial train
Chaunting the Mufes' facred ftrain,
In robes of ceremony dreffed,
With facerdotal ftole and veft,
Each Actor holding Shakefpeare's page,
The *priefts* and rubrick of the ftage.
Such as our thefpian faith requires,
Not begging monks and wandering friars.

Then

† Midfum. Night's Dream.

‡ A proceffion of priefts chaunting high mafs, is
fometimes of wonderful efficacy againft ghofts and goblins, who, whatever profeffion they might have followed
when alive, have, after their corporeal death as great
an averfion to high mafs and all Church ceremonies as
any Calvinift in Scotland.

* Then in a burning chauldron's blaze,
Throw Reynolds's and Morton's plays,
Each page of Allingham's and Cobbe's,
And heavy Boaden's clumfy jobs ;
The infane verfe, and madder profe
Of Lewis, Coleman's puppet-fhows—
And all the trafh the German's fend here
Thro' Thompfon, Noeden, Plumtree, Render,
Be all on the buzaglo placed,
Pacts with the demon of falfe-tafte.

† Next gather in a chryftal bowl
The tears down Pity's cheeks that roll,

H 2 That

* Les exorciftes impoferent filence aux diables, on jetta dans le feu *les pactes* les uns après les autres. Hift. du proces d'Urb. Grand. This liberal and enlightened operation was performed in prefence of fome of the chief men of the Church and of the law, in the year 1631, in now atheift land of France.

† Of the fuppofed effects of luftration no one can be ignorant—I hope ours is conducted *dans les formes.*

That from the riven bofom flow,
Touched by the wand of tragic woe;
Scatter the bleffed drops around,
And fanctify the holy ground;
No envious fiends their footfteps fet
On earth that Pity's tear has wet.

'Tis done—the folemn rites are paid
And Cenfure's in the ocean laid.

And now from fair Augufta's towers
Collect, dear J——s, your fcenic powers;
Not mere allies * that play a fcore
Of nights, " and then are heard no more,"
That for a moment fhine, and then
To darknefs give us up again;—

Not

*I had rather never fee a good actor on our ftage, than fee him only for a few nights, which only ferve to throw the reft of the feafon into a deeper night—

Et obtentâ denfantur nocte tenebræ.

Nor fhould it be forgotten, that thefe ftrangers are birds of prey as well as of paffage.

Not mummers fit to pleafe the gallery,
Collected at a five pound‡ falary;—
Not *Poucets* to fay parts by rote,—
Not fingers who can't fing a note.
Drive from your ftage all foreign nonfenfe,
And fhows that only pleafe at one fenfe—
Trafh that ufurps the comic name,
Mad farce and maudlin melodrame.
Throw off the trammels of the mode,
A fhifting yet a ponderous load;
Nor let your native fenfe and tafte
By others follies be difgraced,

Catch

‡ Imperavit (Marcus Antoninus) etiam *fcenicas* do-
nationes, jubens ut *quinos aureos* fcenici acciperent.
Jul. Cap. in Vit. M. A. Mr. Jones in this point imitates the Roman emperor with a fcrupulous accuracy,
as he never gives a higher falary than 5l. per week. In
London they give 10l. 15l. and 20l.—Surely it would be
(as the tradefmen fay) *worth his while* to give *two* or
three good actors here, as much as they can get elfe-
where.

Catch timid merit as it fprings,

Give to your * liberal foul full wings,

The ftages golden age reftore,

And Cenfure fhall return no more. †

* Mr. Jones's liberality is a favourite topic of expa-
tiation amongft his friends, and I believe not unjuftly ;
but I intreat him to exercife it in procuring a few good
players for the Theatre Royal, an expedient of generofity which he has not yet practifed to any confiderable extent.

† Gentle reader who haft travelled thefe *fix* heavy
ftages thro' with me, accept my thanks for the patience,
with which you have borne the roughnefs of the road,
and the miftakes and wanderings of our courfe, " beg-
gar that I am, I'm poor even in thanks" and have no
other reward to offer, than, that I affure you, I fhall
not again trefpafs on your kindnefs and good nature—
valete, and if you can *plaudite.*

FINIS.

ERRATA.

Preface, page xi. line 23 for ποςήσιν read ποιησιν.

Page 1 line 8 for *directs* read *direct.*

21 — 17 dele *in.*

30 — 17 for *parciunt* read *parcunt.*

37 — 90 after *atque* dele ;

41 — 15 for *perugue* read *peruque.*

46 — 14 for *tædere* read *lædere.*

47 — 3 for ΑΛΝ   read ΑΕΝ.

58 — 2 for *virture* read *virtue.*

————

Two or *three* perfons will difcover *two* or *three* errors in the Greek accentuation, for which the Printer humbly craves forgivenefs.

THE AMAZONIAD;

OR,

Figure and Fashion:

A

SCUFFLE IN HIGH LIFE.

WITH

NOTES CRITICAL AND HISTORICAL,

INTERSPERSED WITH

Choice Anecdotes of Bon Ton.

———

" Makes female worthies, in their works,

" To fight like Termagants and Turks."

HUDIBRAS.

———

Dublin :

PRINTED BY JOHN KING,

No. 2, Westmoreland-Street,

———

1806,

THE AMAZONIAD;

OR

FIGURE AND FASHION,

&c.

ADVERTISEMENT.

I AM sensible, gentle Reader, of the boldness of the present undertaking in which I, an obscure and humble individual, have embarked.—I have presumed, for your instruction and delight, to draw aside the silken curtains which, like those interposed before a naked Venus, conceal the mysteries of high life from profane eyes. I know, that, in ancient times, those, who revealed the great mysteries of certain female deities, were held in extreme abhorrence and marked for execration among the initiated:

> " Vetabo qui Cereris Sacrum
> " Vulgarit," &c.   HOR.

I am conscious that I shall draw upon me the tongues, and perhaps the talons of many dis-

B

tinguished male and female Characters. Some
will think that I have said too much about them;
some that I said too little; others will be perfectly indignant that they have been wholly
omitted. *Non est nostrum tantas componere
lites.* Thy improvement, Reader, was my
only object, to that I postponed all other con-
siderations. I know thou wilt be wonderfully
edified, by the knowledge of high life, the
examples of courtly politeness, female virtue,
and heroic worth here recorded.

It may perhaps surprize many, that a person,
removed like me from the Cabinets of the great
and the Boudoirs of the fair, should be able to
acquire a knowledge of such high matters.
People may be led to question the authenticity
of the relations here given, but I pledge myself
for the veracity and fidelity of the Narratives:
and the surprize of my Reader will cease, when
he shall be told, what infinite pains I have taken
to procure information. I have searched
every corner where knowledge was to be
found.—I have assumed various disguises to
facilitate my enquiries.—I have worn out many

pair of Shoes and Boots, and expended many
Shillings in Coach-hire.—I have frequented
Levees in the Uniform of the Church and the
Army.—I have attended Balls and Routs,
sometimes as a fashionable Lounger, sometimes
in the costume of an old Lady.—I have made
myself by turns a Porter, a Chairman, a powdered Footman, a Chimney Sweeper, a Sheriff's
Bailiff, and a Parish Watchman, that I might
the more readily insinuate myself, by night
and by day, into places where whispers might
be overheard, and anecdotes of secret History
might be gleaned. I have even intrigued with
Chamber Maids, to obtain from those faithful
repositories of secrecy the information I de-
sired. I have even done more, (Heaven for-
give me !)—I have resorted to the Black art,
and called up *Spirits from the vasty deep*, to
bring me Information. The fruit of all my
labours and all my perils is now before the
Reader: and I am sure will be equally useful
with the labours of Mr. Kelly, who teaches
Ladies to manage their Hoops. I am sensible,
that to my invisibility, or rather to the variety

of forms in which I have appeared, I must
owe my security from a nest of Hornets, who
would swarm about my ears, and sting me to
the quick.—Many guesses at my person will be
made; but made in vain. It will be as easy to
guess the true Author of *Pursuits of Literature.*
Many Writers, stung with envy, will take up
the pen; and perhaps some innocent persons
may suffer, and be marked out as the object of
personal attack, which I see with sorrow, and
lament to say, is too much the fashion in the
present ill-natured times. It is really shock-
ing to see what a crop of these prickly weeds
the rank soil of *Dublin* has produced!—*Familiar Epistles to the Manager, Cutcha Cutchoo,*
(do I spell the word properly?) *The Metropolis*
in many Cantos, *Modest Reply by the Manager,* so called, as *Lucus a non lucendo,* from
its being immodest, not that I suppose Mr.
Jones really wrote the *Modest Reply.* All or
any of the Authors of these may be disposed
to attack the supposed Author of this Heroico-
fashionable Poem, delighted with the idea of
starting new Game.

That the Reader may the better understand the following Poem, it is necessary to advert to the circumstance which gave occasion to its composition. On a night, when a play was ordered by the Lord Lieutenant; the Lady of the C******** ** ***** *pro tempore* demanded, as her right, the box opposite to that in which his Excellency sits on these occasions. This claim was however contended with great heat, by the Lady of a very exalted ** ******** herself a person of quality.—The pretensions of the latter were urged with so much ardour and pertinacity, that the military Lady, after almost as great a defence as that the Prince of *Hesse* now makes in *Gaeta*, was obliged to capitulate, and evacuate the box, not however without stipulating for the free and undisturbed possession of the box adjoining, the prior occupant of which was ejected to make room for her, who in turn displaced the next neighbour, until a general dislocation of the solids prevailed, through all the Theatric system, as was learnedly observed by my dear and very good friend *Doctor Hill.*

B 3

This is a great and auspicious æra, *Magnus ab integro seclorum nascitur Ordo.* Many a high subject of heroic song croud on the enraptured imagination of the astonished Bard, and if Providence spares me life, I shall endeavour to do justice to them. In the mean time, I beg leave, with all humility, to inscribe these first fruits of my Heroical Lucubrations to the Gallant and Noble Gentlemen who frequent the *Board of Green Cloth.*

FIGURE AND FASHION, &c.

FIRST CANTO.

ARGUMENT.

*SUBJECT proposed—Invocation—Arrival of the Duke and Duchess—Their great popularity—Joy of the people—To gratify them a play is performed by command—Liberality of the Manager on the occasion—Eagerness of the people to obtain places in the Playhouse—Compared to the eager application for places on a change of ministry—The crowds in the lobby besieging and beseeching Mr. M'Nally—Dennira appears—Description of her person—Apostrophe to the G******—Dennira's address to Mr. M'Nally—He at first grants her request—Appearance of a competitor—Surprize of every body—Attended by the mace—Law argument of Philothemis to prove that it would be treason, or at least sedition, not to give her the box—Threatens M'Nally with Major S---.—He runs away in a fright—Great confusion—War inevitable—Portents and prodigies.*

FIGURE AND FASHION;

OR,

THE HEROINES.

———

Wহ্WHAT mighty rage the female heart inflames,
How rivalship embroils ambitious dames,
Whose mighty deeds eclipse the warlike praise
Of stoutest Amazons in ancient days,
And all that modern bards have sung or said, 5
Of bright *Clorinda* and the *Gallic* maid :*
How female bosoms glow with love of place,
The General's truncheon clashing with the mace,
I tell.—Old Father *Liffey* hears the song ;
His echoes shall the martial notes prolong.   10
And thou, whose waters emblematic crawl
Thro' dirt and darkness to the Castle wall,
Thou *Poddle* † hear ; and as they labouring flow,
Thro' many a sewer and aqueduct below,
Delay their march, attentive to the sound,   15
And irrigate each vault and kitchen round.

———

* Joan of Arc.

† The River Poddle winds under ground from near the
old Episcopal Palace to the Castle.

And yet, the Muse recoils from such a strain,
The simple mate of rustics on the plain,
Confin'd to themes that rural manners yield;
The match of ploughing in the furrow'd field,   20
The show of cattle, mighty bulls and boars,
Rams, ewes, and wethers, hoggets, lambs, and stores.
Or if to sing of warriors was her care,
She never rose beyond a country fair.
But how the feuds of polish'd life to sing!   25
The Poet's fingers tremble on the string.
He feels how rashly he has pushed from shore,
In open bark, without a sail or oar.
What hand from ship-wreck shall preserve his fame ?
What influence aid him in the daring aim ?   30
The hereditary harp, O M*****, try,
And tune for me prelusive minstrelsy ;
Then shall my numbers please each courtly ear,
And ev'n a Duchess shall vouchsafe to hear.
To thee, great arbiter of Elegance   35
In concerts, sermons, plays, and mazy dance,
The Muse appeals. With powerful aid support
This new attendant on a Viceroy's court.
Whether reclined in the viceregal coach,   *
Or thron'd more airy in the gilt baroach,   40

* " Whether you take Cervantes' serious air,
  " Or nod and shake in Rabelais' easy chair." Pope.

Lend thine assurance to the bashful bard,
So may lawn sleeves the charity reward.
Meantime let oily *Joe* * the bagpipe sound,
And Ord'nance stores re-echo all around.
Then shall a laureat's name the bard adorn,　　45
And crown of bays by ancient *Gorgey* borne.

'Twas at the time, when *Russell's* noble son
Had prostrate *Erin's* faded sceptre won:
Our loud acclaims a people's hope confest,
And frantic pleasure hail'd the high-born guest.　50
With fond delight the partial croud descry
The nose heroic and commanding eye. †
With fond delight thro' ev'ry line they trace
How *Russell* virtues animate his face.
Brisk as a fairy, volatile as air,　　55
The bonny Duchess, blithe and debonnair;
Boast of the *Highland* clans, old *Scotia's* pride,
In youthful vigour grac'd the Viceroy's side.

* Mr A——. the preceding treasurer of the Ordnance
retired on his full salary to make room for him.

† Imitated from Addison——
　"In every stroke, in every line,
　"See some exalted virtue shine,
　"And Albion's happiness we trace
　"In every feature of his face."

Still as she pass'd, the choral song arose,
Success to the Duchess wherever she goes.   60
What crowds prest forward as affection led,
And eager eyes with ceaseless gazing fed.

   To satisfy the wishes of the land,
A comedy was ordered " by Command ;"
That happy *Teague* might revel in delight,   65
And at the Viceroy stare a live-long night;
For, be it mentioned underneath the rose,
All savages are fond of raree shows.
The thrifty Manager, tho' cook profest, *
Was poz'd to cater for the scenic feast.   70
For, sooth to say, full many a barn affords
A better company than tramp his boards.
Then Heaven enlarg'd, O J——s, thy frugal mind,
To glad with 'bounty all the vassal kind.
He added ten pence to their weekly pay, †   75
And ev'ry spouter had two meals that day.

* * * * * * *

   * The culinary talents of this gentleman have been
celebrated by other writers, much yet remains unsung.

   † Lest commentators should be in doubt an hundred years
hence, why ten pence was the precise modicum added,
you are to know it was on account of the most current
coin at that time—ten-penny tokens. The pittance allowed
at present to performers in Dublin, is well calculated to

Good jockies all are in the rule agreed,
To work their horses well, and well to feed :
By different maxims human brutes we treat,
Man sorely toils and sparingly should eat.   80
This sage advice the manager retains,
And meagre diet through the green room reigns.

No sooner was the gracious purpose known,
Than Expectation travell'd o'er the town
On flapping wings, and call'd the grave, the gay,85
To meet their new chief ruler at the play.
Sure never glow'd in opposition breast,
Such love of place as then the croud possest.
Say, hast thou levied in the changeful hour,
Some party leader, newly call'd to pow'r ?   90
Say, hast thou marked how visages impart
The greedy wishes and the throbbing heart ?
Say, hast thou stood th' expectant crowd among,
That E****** anti-room, on Fridays throng ;
And bar and army seen, and church and state,   95
With anxious awe their oracle await ?

qualify them for acting ghosts.   The players are not
unaptly called Vassal train, to express the sovereign authority exercised by his Most Despotic Highness the Manager.
C

Then, Reader, some faint notion might be form'd
How hope and fear the public bosom storm'd.
Then might'st thou judge what eager, throbbing hearts,
What loud pretensions and what cringing arts, 100
The great, the little show'd, the high, the low,
The belle, the punk, the citizen, the beau.
There *Corcorans, Keenaghans, Mullowneys* came,
Burns, Killaughers, Shaughnessys well known to fame,
M'Laughlins, Dempsys, Murphys, Moonies urged
    their claim.   105
Round *Macanally* prest a mingled croud,
Liberal in promise, in petition loud ;
All begging places, for by heaven's decree,
The Castle Spectre * of that house was he.
Amid the lobby he majestic stands,   110
The sheet'† portentous trembling in his hands :
He hears their claims, their merits he debates,
Inspects the mystic leaf, and sings their fates ;

~~~~~~

* A kind of Deity much worshipped by the wild Irish,
and which is supposed to have the power of looking into
futurity and telling fortunes. Its temple is situated between two banking houses and the Irish treasury.

† Sheet—A large Chart on which the Ichnography of the
Boxes is delineated, and according to which they are
engaged from the box-keeper.

Some he receives, and sternly some repels,
These grief o'erwhelms, those exultation swells. 115
Thus, on the bank of *Styx* when *Charon* stood,
And shades by myriads sought to pass the flood, *
Some he rejected, some to pass allow'd,
And grief and joy alternate filled the crowd.

Let every head in adoration bow,   120
Let all the crowd superiour claims allow;
And all confess in that portentous hour,
The sovereign sway of beauty's magic power.
From right to left † ye beaus and belles recede,
Her high pretensions let *Dennira* plead.   125
What eastern harams brighter charms contain,
Than *Liffey's* banks can shew, and *Erin's* plain?
O, happy General, tho' the swarthy east
The prowess of thy conqu'ring arm confest;

---

* " Stabant orantes primi transmittere cursum,
" Tendebantque manus Ripæ ulterioris amore.
" Navita sed tristis nunc hos, nunc accipit illos,
" Ast alios longe submotos arcet arenâ." VIRGIL.

† Right to left——The author here shews consummate
judgment, *Scit reddere convenientia cuique*——when he comes
to speak of a General's Lady, and describe the croud making
way for her, he employs terms applicable to military
evolutions.

C 2

Mysore and *Tanjore*, *Gauts* and rivers past,   130
How poor were all thy conquests to the last!
In her embrace more treasure he explores,
Than *lacs* uncounted and unnumbered *crores* :*
Behold her eyes, and mark how dimly shine
Thine emeralds, *Gani*, and *Golconda's* mine;   135.
Corn, wine, and oil her beauteous looks expand,
And seem to call us to the promis'd land.
Like *Ceres* rich, in gladsome triumph borne,
Or Plenty's Goddess, but without a horn :
What pow'r of words her tempting charms may reach,
Firm as an apple, juicy as a peach.   141
Like the full moon, her face resplendant shows,
Her breasts are hillocks crown'd with living snows.
———————— the modest muse no farther pries,
The citadel is kept for soldier eyes.†   145
With smiles that prefac'd ev'ry word she spoke,
From coral lips persuasive accents broke:
" *Muc*, honest fellow, I the box engage,
" That fronts the Viceroy's and adjoins the stage ;

———————

* Lacs and Crores— Indian terms for sums of money.

† I cannot sufficiently admire the discretion of the poet
in drawing in the reins of imagination which else might
have run away with him at full gallop, into the Paradise of
Mahomet and all the luxuriance of *Asiatic* description —Gauts
mountain passes to the hill country.

" The General to the Viceroy should be near, 150
" Flame in the van or sparkle in the rear;
" This post, dear Devil, let thy care defend,
" And I, by Heav'n, for ever am thy friend;
" Thy next review * shall own my fostering aid,
" To thy support I'll march a whole brigade." 155
Such charms, such accents might a God have caught,
Much more, a man of fleshly substance wrought.
The sheet he view'd, he seiz'd the ready quill,
And mark'd the station at the charmer's will.
The charmer curtsey'd with commanding grace, 160
And conscious triumph flush'd her lovely face.
But ah, how frail and transient man's delight!
How soon the fairest morn is clos'd in night!
Brief the possession of all human things,
Doubtful the fate of beauties and of kings. 165
Pass some few days, *Dennira* shall lament
The hour *M'Nally* gave his rash consent.

* Meaning, perhaps, the Box-keeper's Benefit.

† " Nescia mens hominum fati sortisque futuræ,
" Et servare modum, rebus sublata secundis.
" Turno tempus erit, magno cum optaverit emptum
" Intactum Pallanta; et cum spolia ista diemque
" Oderit." Virgil.

C 3

Think not thy conquest sure, triumphant dame,
A mighty rival shall dispute the claim.

   " Make way, make way there," thro' the lobby
       sounds ;   170
The stately mace th' astonished crowd confounds.
With winning smile, conciliatory grace,
Then gentle D**** display'd his pleasant face. *
Symbol of Justice, when the mace they saw,
The crowd retir'd with reverential awe.   175
Shrill menaces are heard, and words of ire,
With eyes indignant and with cheeks of fire,
A dame advanc'd impetuous to the charge ;
In form not ample, but in spirit large.
Thus *Tydeus* in a narrow compass show'd   180
What mighty virtues in his bosom glow'd.
An high-born worth her conscious looks exprest,
Th' astonished Box-keeper she thus addrest :
" Are Rules of Equity acknowledged here ?
" For this Decree, do precedents appear?   185

* A gentleman of prepossessing looks and manners, of
singular urbanity and singleness of heart. It must gratify
the public to know, that he has accumulated an estate of
four or five thousand a year, through the mere blessing of
Providence on disinterested virtue, without any exertion
of his own.

" Ere your Injunction* shall possess the dame ;

" Let a Petitioner re-hearing claim.

" *Philothemis* my Name, in Heaven enroll'd,

" The mace of justice in my grasp I hold.—

" Say, shall the truncheon with the mace contend ?

" To Martial Law, shall Courts of Justice bend ?191

" To back my wishes I *Papinian* bring,

" He keeps the conscience of our Lord the King.

" His *Irish* conscience, for the Laws decide,

" He has a conscience on the other side,   195

" And *Erskine* keeps it ; but what Fate allows

" To *Teague* and *Pat* is guarded by my spouse.

" When *Æolus* the wind in bags confin'd,

" To wise *Ulysses* he the charge assigned.

" Thus in a purse, our gracious King imparts,   200

" His seal'd-up conscience to some man of arts.

* There is great beauty in this passage; the character is admirably preserved. As *Dennira* had used Military terms, so the fair and noble pleader shows much technical knowledge. When a Decree has been obtained, an Injunction goes to put the party in possession. Before a Decree is enrolled, a re-hearing is granted on petition. I refer the female reader to *Mitford's* Chancery Practice, for information on this abstruse subject.

" If to the Sovereign conscience should be near,

" Near should it's Keeper be ; not day so clear.

" And what disloyal tongue shall dare to say,

" The King can ever from his conscience stray ?*205

" Seditious is the wretch, who would divide,

" The conscience-keeper from the Sovereign's side.

" It tends to raise suspicions most unjust,

" It tends to fill the public with distrust.

" The purse and seal be ever full in view,   210

" That all may know the people have their due.

" I, as their keeper's half, should near be found

" To Sovereign's Delegate, on *Irish* ground.

" And she who would exclude me from my place,

" Would Law resist and Government disgrace.   215

" 'Tis contumacy, 'tis contempt of Court.—

" Serjeant at Arms, my dignity support.—

" In such a Cause, I'll make a mighty stir,

" And call in M******, call in Major S** "

* Such is the maxim of the Law—the King can do no wrong. The argument of the Lady is close and unanswerable. The King can do no wrong, therefore is inseparable from his conscience, *ergo* inseparable from the keeper of it, his C****** *** *ergo* inseparable from the C*********'s wife, who is the better half of the C*********, *ergo* he who separates the C*********'s wife from the King would separate the King and his conscience, or insinuate that they may be separated, and is no good subject.—Q. E. D.

These words of terror acted like a spell.—　220
As at the appearance of some Fiend of Hell,
Pale and aghast poor *Macanally* stands,
The pen and ink now glided from his hands.—
He tore the sheet, he vanished in a fright,
Murmuring, and with him-fled the shades of night.—
His flight so sudden, all the croud divides,　226
Perplexed they range, the Door-keepers their guides.
The House was all before them, where to choose;
But who shall grant them Boxes, or refuse;
Awhile they hesitate, awhile they pause,　230
Then brutal force supplies the place of Laws.—

Unnumber'd Portents, dreadful and deform,
Announc'd the rising of a fatal storm.—
Pease fell in torrents, Goblins danc'd in air,
With flashing Rosin, Stage and Green Room glare.
Along the lofts terrific thunder roll'd,　236
The Catcall scream'd, the Bell of *Jaffier* toll'd.
Untouch'd by any hand, the Basses roar,
Masques move, without their heads, along the floor.
From every trap-door Demons rise to view,　240
And Sisters weird th' infernal Chaldron brew.
Exulting discord hail'd the loud alarms,
And all the combatants prepare for arms.

But now 'tis time to rest my wearied steed,
Another song shall bid the war proceed.*   245

───────

* See the description of the prodigies that announced the death of Julius Cæsar.——Virgil's Georgics, Book the First.

END OF THE FIRST CANTO.

FIGURE AND FASHION; &c.

SECOND CANTO.

FIGURE AND FASHION;

OR,

THE HEROINES.

———

SECOND CANTO.

To all that in the pale of Fashion dwell,
The Blade of spirit, and the lively Belle,
To all the lounging, simp'ring, idle Crew,
That yawn and languish still for something new,
Or gape, like Oysters, in the Tide of Time,   5
For what it brings, the Author sends his Rhyme.—
Think not, dear Ladies, think not, gentle Squires,
That malice prompts him, or resentment fires;
Nor, while he paints, by wand'ring Fancy led,
Apply the Cap to any private Head;   10
Like wise Ulysses I for knowledge strayed,
And various Scenes and Characters survey'd.
Tho' living Forms Imagination warm,
Beshrew my Heart if I intend you harm!
I seize the Harp, I call the ready Muse,   15
What Bard a Theme so tempting could refuse?
What Knights and Sages, from *Britannia* borne,
What peerless Dames a *Russell's* Court adorn!

D

Auspicious days await this happy Land.

See the *Green Cloth* forgotten cates expand.[*]   20

On Castle Guard, to chear the Captain's toil,

And light each Ensign's features, with a smile.

While courteous Knights I consecrate to fame

And sing the triumphs of each courtly Dame.

Dear to the sovereigns of the tuneful nine,[†]   25

His sapient ear, may letter'd Y***** incline.

Could my poor Muse, like thee, O! Y***** indite

At once prescriptions and addresses write,

I should not then, thro' many a street and lane,

With strolling minstrels pour an abject strain :   30

My song might hope to reach a viceroy's ear,

Smooth [‡] chaplains sing, and future bishops hear.

Illustrious citizen of *Bedford* town,

Grac'd with square cap, and aldermanic gown,

In solemn token of thy twofold station,   35

High plac'd in *Pæan's* hall, and corporation :

Oh, could he light, like F——s, his visage up,

And tinge his features in a double cup ;

———————

[*] The Board of Green Cloth, which has been long disused, was restored.

[†] Apollo, God of physic as well as of poetry.

[‡] I mean no accusation here against their manhood.

Or could he boast eternal bloom like *V——e*,
For thee the poet to the pipe should dance. * 40
Mean time from us, indulgent sage, receive
Such humble honours as the land may give:
Thrice welcome from the joys that *Bedford* yields,
To deep potations and potatoe fields:
Thrice welcome, to the land of drizzling fogs,
Bulls, blunders, *Galilæans*, and mad dogs.　　46
Oh pious soul, in meek submission, he
Bows to high heaven's omnipotent decree: †
Oh say what station shall his wand'rings close?
In what snug corner shall his age repose?　　50
Whether his talents Providence may call,
To shine the ranger of *Lock* Hospital;

———————

* Let not the author be misunderstood—He means no
unclean allusion to the professional pursuits and applications
of the Doctor, as though the poet of his praise should be put
in sudden motion by the operation of a C——r Pipe,
that would be a silly, preposterous, and misplaced joke—a
joke *a posteriori—minus aptus acutis naribus horum hominum.*

† With submissive resignation to the sovereign comp-
troller of events, could the pious *M——* say more if he
were appointed at last to the twice promised and long expected Bishopric?

Or make him taster of Vaccine infection,
Or president of Digital collection. *
For thee the College honours due prepares,   55
Install thee high in their professor's chairs;
Diplomas they in pill-boxes bestow,
And hemlock garlands wreath, to crown thy brow.
For thee, they meditate such civic feast, †
As sons of *Pæan* only can digest: 60
For thee, with castor-oil, their sallads brew,
With asafœtida enrich the stew:
With manna, squills, they mix nectarious hoard,
And draughts of ether circle round the board.
For thee, mephitic gas in clouds shall roll,   65
And vital air shall impregnate the bowl:
For thee —— but turn my muse, recount the fray,
The ladies chide thee for thy long delay.

* Gathering Digitalis or Fox glove—The apothecaries of
Dublin assemble for the purpose, at a certain time of the year,
and repair to a pass in the mountains called the *Scalp*, where
the plant is found.

† As there was a great round of cabinet dinners, on a
certain late change, to drink success to the new administration, so, there was a great round of medical, surgical, and
apothecarial dinners, to welcome the Doctor to *Ireland*, and
drink a *feverish spring*, a *sickly summer*, and *aguish autumn*,—pia
vota! they had all the good things above enumerated, with
many other dainties prepared according to the *London Art o
Cookery*— *Pharmacopæia Londinensis.*

As the cold north pours forth her barb'rous sons,
Vandals, and *Alans, Lombards, Goths,* and *Huns;** 75
Delicious climes invite the savage mind;
They come like locusts, warping on the wind.
An uncouth deluge o'er the castle spread,
A desperate Town Clerk these invaders led :
Grocers and cooks were there, a rabble rout,
With sturdy vintners, as their liquor stout ;
There fierce attornies struck with wild afright
The peer insolvent and the bankrupt knight ;
For Castle suppers they so keen were set,
Ev'n cutlers came, their appetite to whet.† 80
Not more tumultuous take their noisy way
Voters to hustings, on election day.
With greater rage the *Poddle* never rose,
With filth and foam redundant as it goes,
O'er-spread the kitchens with impetuous sway, 85
And swept the cates and delicates away.

* " A multitude like which the populous north poured
" never from her frozen loins to pass *Rhene* or the *Danaw,*
" when her barbarous sons

" Came like a deluge on the south, and spread
" Beneath *Gibralter* to the *Lybian* sands." MILTON.

† Sir *Charles Vernon* blunted the edge of their appetite,
not with a *billet doux* but *billet amer,* or *lettre de cachet.*

The Castle dames in tender accents moan'd,
The Castle chaplains in the spirit groaned.
Then bold Sir C———s was rous'd with holy zeal,
The wounded honour of the state to feel;   90
Sir C———s distinguish'd for equestrian feat,
From horsemanship yet aching in his seat;
For there had Y—— his healing hand apply'd,
And loss of skin, diachylon supply'd. *
Not greater zeal the christian knight inflam'd 95
At *Acre* when the *Corsican* he tam'd.
Th' enchanted spear he seized with puissant hand,
And drove th' unhallow'd crew from holy land.

Yet undistinguishing his fury chas'd †
Some that ev'n regal drawing-rooms had grac'd. 100
Merchants themselves are chac'd, incongruous
          thought,
From scenes where thousands have been sold and
          bought.

~~~~~~

* The Dutchess insisted that Sir C—— should attend her
on horse-back on an excursion. He remonstrated, and de-
clared on the faith of a true knight, he had never rode in his
life. Her Grace answered, it was time he should begin.—
No excuse would be admitted. He was set on a fiery
charger.—But this adventure deserves a separate poem.

† " Who can be wise, amazed, temperate, and furious, loyal,
" and neutral in a moment ?——No man." SHAKESPEARE.

Alas, Sir *John*, * how tears my utterance drown!
Accomplish'd Scriv'ner, is thy worth unknown?
Art thou excluded? let the Viceroy look,   105
Mark thine establishment, thy Gallic cook.
'Tis piteous, Oh! thee *G——h* † I bewail.—
Are brilliant buckles then of no avail?
Thy mein so sweet, demeanour so polite,
Thy wig so flaxen, and thy face so white! 110
Dress and address like thine might well comport
With silken circles in the crowded court.
Ev'n *F——g* was ‡ rejected, form'd by fate,
A *Tuscan* column to sustain the state;

---

* This is a just anticipation, generally adopted, and in-
dicatory of the public sense of this accomplished and polite
attorney's high deserts and pretensions. He is not yet
knighted, but he has long been the companion of the
great and noble. He is truly a consequential man. The
term scrivener seems to have been admitted for the sake
of the rhyme, not in contempt of this most important
attorney.

† A *Belle Esprit* of an uncommon ease and elegance in his
manners. He had fair pretensions to be receceived at the
Castle by prescription, as he was formerly a member of the
Irish Parliament and must have dined at the alphabet
dinners.

‡ The admirable Creighton of the Attorney's Corps. I have
seen him preside at a court martial with real dignity.

Strange versatility, in one combin'd,   113
Th' attorney's pen is with a laurel twin'd !
He bids discordant aims in one agree,
Captain, philosopher, and agent he :
Now great *tactician* marches to the Park,
Now, like Sir *Isaac*, solves some problem dark, 120
Now lifts his eye to count the starry host,
Now pores discreetly on a bill of cost :
The range of science there his cares enlarge,
He swells the catalogue, augments the charge.

This feat atchiev'd, loud *Io Pean* sound,   125
Trophies are rais'd, the vaulted roofs rebound :
And while the victors revell'd in delight,
A galaxy of lamps emblaz'd the night.
In solemn pomp, their triumphs to declare,
Now, for the theatre the crowd prepare.   130
Say, Muse, their names then known, who first, who
        last,
To *Crow-Street*, with the Castle Spectre past.*

* The Secretary is considered as the domestic genius, the
Lar or household God of the Castle, therefore, the crowd
is with peculiar propriety made to follow him, particularly
as there was a great demand for *places* at this juncture.

He, as expectants various fates impell,

Brings with him " airs from heav'n and blasts from
    hell."

Pale tho' he glares, yet him you never meet 135

Burst from his *cerements* in a winding sheet.

Nor yet with saucer eye the crowd he daunts,

In silks and sattins drawing-rooms he haunts.

His wardrobe lilac velvets can afford,

The star-bright buttons, and the studded sword; 140

Far other weeds than deck the shadowy host,

Or furnish out the toilet of a Ghost :

With plumage nodding, and with fans display'd,

The gay seducer led the cavalcade.

When thro' the streets his daily walk he takes, 145

Each female heart with tender tumult akes,

The Balconies are throng'd with fond delight,

And ladies call the youth the pavement knight.*

---

* I need not dwell on the character here introduced, not
to know him would argue my Reader unknown, no visitant
at the Castle, no inmate of polite houses—But if this poem
should fall into the hands of the vulgar and ignorant, contrary to my intentions, I will condescend to refer them for
further information to a publication, called *Familiar Epistles,*
and ascribed to one hundred different authors.

Full in the van Sir C———r appears,
A coat of blazon on his back he bears. *   150
Then came Sir C——, by nature form'd in sport,
The harmless Zany of a merry court.
O heav'n-taught chamberlain, so born and bred,
With grace to light the ladies up to bed; †
To see their secrets with no tell-tale eye;   155
Lay on their rouge, and their cosmetics buy:
Some forty birth-days added let him see,
And what *Polonius* was, shall *V*—— be.
Next good Sir *G*——, ordained Sir *C*——'s aid,
In doing nothing, (as by Teague 'tis said).   160
In second childhood, of a green old age,
In years like *Nestor*, but not quite as sage.

———————

* *Ulster King at Arms*, a necessary person on this occasion, to marshal the triumphal procession, to proclaim the victory over the *Goths* and *Vandals*, and to declare war with them according to the terms and stipulations of the *red and black lists* and *Joyeuse Entrée* of the Castle. Sir *C*—— keeps his shop of honours and College of arms in the house formerly occupied by Mrs. *Mayne*, better known by the name of *Sally M'Laine*.

† The term *Grace* here most happily admits of a double sense to denote not only the elegance of manner, but the purity of intention, with which this carpet knight, dubb'd with un-hack'd rapier, performs his various and confidential carnival functions.

He, shallow as the babbling * brook, enjoys
His own anility of ceaseless noise.
There H——† was found from the seraglio drawn,
By love of Novelty and love of Lawn.   166
No fairer youth the *Bosphorus* survey'd,
No fairer youth with *Saint Sophia* stray'd ;
Soft was his speech, seducing were his airs,
Most meet for bed-chambers, or state affairs.   170
C————*h*, entitled by paternal strain,
To tell th' Exchequer, nor to tell in vain,
Was there, ‡ more proud of Ensign's novel rank,§
Than were he crown'd Director of the Bank.
Next *M*—— who bewails, with tearful eye,   175
That dying Prelates will not wholly die.

* So Grey in his Elegy—
  " His listless length at noon-tide would he stretch,
  " And pore upon the brook that babbles by."

† Commentators conjecture that this passage is descriptive
of a young Abbe of fair hopes, who had formerly a situation
in the Embassy to *Constantinople*. Quere—Whether *lawn*
here means lawn *Shifts* or lawn *Sleeves?*

‡ There was in former ages, when Pigs were Swine, a
certain Sir Henry who had a finger in the Treasury pie. In his
accounts was a certain *Hiatus valde deflendus*.

§ The rank of Ensign newly bestowed to qualify him to be
Aid du Camp.

May'st thou no second disappointment know,

But live to bury *Limerick* or *Raphoe:*

Then might'st thou shine, in mitred carriage borne,

And grace lawn sleeves,* as thee lawn sleeves adorn.

With nose upturn'd and reconnoitring eyes,†   181

Intent to seize our blunders as they rise,

The vanity, the stupid admiration,

And aukward flattery, of our foolish nation ;‡

And food purvey for hourly ridicule,   185

From tones and gestures of each *Irish* fool.

Now simp'ring, now with sly sardonic grin,

That spoke the n ovements of contempt within,

Came S—— *F*—— tempting to the view,

Of Sphynx the features, with an Æthiop's hue. 190

A bouncing charmer, fit to deal with man,

And wrestle fairly on the *Spartan* plan.

With these a body of alluring Dames,

'Twould ask a *Maro's* muse to sing their names.

---

* " Se qua Fato aspera rumpas
  " Tu Marcellu eris."———

† Omnia suspendens naso adunco, is the motto of these witty Ladies, who cut and carve the foolish, blundering Irish, at an unmerciful rate.

‡ More foolish in nothing than in their indiscriminate Hospitality to Strangers, who laugh at them and their disregard of their own country.

Cornets and Chaplains, shallow, pert and vain, 195
The living lumber of a Viceroy's train.
All these and more in state to *Crow-street* haste,
The swinish many wonder'd as they past:
For since the UNION, to that glorious day,
They had not seen a cavalcade so gay ;   200
Henchmen, and Pages, Footmen all a row,
With gentlemen at large, a goodly show ;
Coaches, and chariots,* gorgeous liveries,
Oh 'twas a sight, to renovate sore eyes.

* That fiction is the soul of Poetry, the honest Author in
the abundance of his love for Truth, must acknowledge, that
it is only by poetic licence that he has made Major *B.* and
Sir *C.* inseparable companions in the Viceregal train.—Truth
is, let them scent and essence themselves, as they will, they
are in bad odour with the bonny Lass. Sir *C.* has incurred
her incurable displeasure by his pious love of Castle etiquette,
and manful resistance to the dancing propensity of the fair
and noble Lady, in defence of ancient ceremonial. She seems
to regard him much as *Sancho* did the dread *Doctor*, with his
wand, or rather as a kind of male *Duenna*, stationed to be a
restraint on mirth, a damper of pleasures. She looks upon
him, as a man of an agreeable absence, whose presence may
well be dispensed with at the private parties where mirth and
jollity—

          " Trip it, as they go,
          " On the light fantastic toe."
Poor *B* poor *C.* virtuous martyrs to the righteous love of
forms. Ye are laid under an interdict—no coach allowed to

E

Now at the Theatre arrived they found   205
In every Box, above, below, around,
Beauty and fashion, all was fair and fine,
The muslins flutter and the jewels shine.
Some of the Names the muses can rehearse,
The rest to memory dead, are lost to verse.   210
There like horn'd Beetle, **** they spy,
With sharp proboscis and with staring eye.
Bulky and huge beside her sate my Lord,
With chops yet wat'ring from the sumptuous board.
Large as some porpoise cast upon the strand,   215
Or *Tityus* stretching o'er a length of land.
A slobbering bib around his neck was dight,
Drops to receive, that savoury smells excite.
Behold their hope, the C—— too advance,
With arts of dress, imported new from *France*.   220
No youth exists of base or noble race,
So just a judge of muslin and of lace.
No youth a neck-cloth ties, with air so smart,
But dear he purchased that important art.
On Gallic shores a Virtuoso taught,   225
The precious secret fifty Pieces bought.

----

carry you—ye are excluded from the private parties, amerced
of the joyous suppers, forced to wear livery ; but to so—
" *Quis talia fando temperet a Lachrymis ?*"

Her Cards awhile fair *M*——— resigns
And ancient *J*——— from the *Austrian* lines, *
Known for the triumphs that *Cassino* brings,
And fam'd in annals of the four great Kings.　　230
And homely *M****** lab'ring to support
Th' imposing airs that suit a place at Court.
His ancient wardrobe *Joseph* then reveal'd,
For ten Olympiads from the sun conceal'd.
Silks, velvets, tabbinets, were all display'd,　　235
Points, laces, fringe, embroidery and brocade.
All hues that in a bed of tulips glow,
And garments more than *Monmouth-street* can show.
Raptur'd he gaz'd—joy elevates his crest—
A lively dress he singled from the rest.　　240
Pea-green the coat—the vest was saxon blue—
The sattin small-cloths were of sable hue.
His silken stockings, which had once been white,
With golden clocks the gazer's eye delight.
His stuccoed head would make a stoic smile,　　245
Of pins an armoury—of curls a pile.
But why should I attempt in humble rhymes,
To paint the finery of other times?

* Not *perpendicular lines*—they are not in the General's
way—but lines military.

E 2

Of H———d stem *Stuarta* there appears,

A noble virgin of twice twenty years.   250

Old R———— too that night her cards resigned,

Of manners vulgar, but of jolly mind.

She* too was there, who left each wond'ring guest,

To seek Viceregal notice at the feast.

The guests indignant saw their hostess fly   255

To pick cold bones with *Van*† and quality :

Her husband bowing cries, (poor civil man)

" My lady wife is fled to lady *Van*."

The mendicant of peerage there they found,

In snows of age, with youthful vices crown'd,   260

Who kept no promise, serv'd no useful end,

Spent princely fortunes, never had a friend.

———————

* It is a most delectable story how the company were
invited on a long notice, by my Lady J———y—how they
all expected a ball and supper, took their measures accordingly, and sent off their carriages and servants, desiring them
to return at three in the morn.—How Lady J———y marched
off to Lady *Van's* ball, to see the Duchess, and left her
caro spose to bow the company out of the house supperless
as well as he could.

† Commentators are in great doubt who is meant by *Van*,
some think *Vanhomrigh*, others *Vansittart*, some *Vannuck*,
some *Vanbutchell*, some *Vandeput*, &c. &c.

There too, with solid everlasting grin,
And all the phlegm of *Holland, Van* was seen,*
A sober youth—but haste ! what dire alarms,   265
Prelusive sound a symphony for arms.
High notes of discord, screams of female rage,
Lament, and menace, now all ears engage.
No trivial causes hostile fury move,
No vulgar combatants their valour prove: 270
Precedence, potent cause, to warfare brings,
Ambitious Females, and contending Kings.
To martial science was *Dennira* train'd,†
She knew how much by vigilance is gained.
Scarce her Videts the doors had open found,   275
She came and seized on the disputed ground.
In books of tactics, and reports she saw
" Possession makes eleven points of law,"

---

* I am in doubt as to the person here meant, perhaps
it may mean some wealthy merchant, or thriving haber-
dasher, perhaps some clerk in a public office, who possesses a
comfortable opacity of intelect, and a moderate knowledge
of vulgar arithmetic.

† It is highly in character that the daughter of an Attorney
and the wife of a General should be train'd in the science of
offence and defence, should know all the value of anticipation,
and be ready to seize on every advantage.

For conversant was she, with modern entries,
And puzzled Lawyers, with *black letter ventries.* 280
Her plumy females in the van appear,
Her garrison battalions guard the rear.
The beauteous leader, in herself a host,
Sate with her flank supported by a post. *
In this position waits the storm, and shows   285
A countenance imposing to the foes.
Nor waited long—for hostile tongues are heard,
And fierce *Philothemis* in force appear'd.
In ancient days, as 'tis by *Homer* sung,
The *Trojan* Bards came on, with clam'rous tongue.
Th' assailants war proclaim, in wrathful tones, 291
" Where is the Box-keeper? say where is *Jones* ?
" Turn out the bold intruder with disgrace ;
" We'll teach the lady to usurp a place."
Never before such balanc'd forces met,   295
For warlike Rubbers so complete a set.
Nor proud *Dennira* to the claim will yield,
Nor will *Philothemis* quit the field.
The fair each moment in their anger rose,
Words lead to words, and blows elicit blows.   300

* This was her *Point D'Appui,* to speak in the military
phrase. But quere, what post ? a military or an architec-
tural post ? a post in the army, or a post under government ?

The Gods above, tho' far from sight remov'd,
With shrilly cat calls aid the din they lov'd.
The powers of discord ruled in frantic mood ;
And stern *Erinnys* dipt her torch in blood.

END OF THE SECOND CANTO.

FIGURE AND FASHION, &c.

THIRD CANTO.

ARGUMENT.

*AUTHOR regrets that the days of Chivalry are no more, and that Ladies are obliged to fight their own battles when questions of Precedence occur.—Fight begins—*Philothemis *attempts to pull* Dennira *from her seat, is foiled in the attempt, throws a bowl of tea in her face—*Dennira's *brave resistance; She drives a half-sucked orange into the mouth of* Philothemis, *who returns discomfited—*Themis *observes this, assumes the semblance of a Six-Clerk, and flies to the Four-Courts for reinforcements—The names of some who came at the call of* Themis—*The battle renewed—*Bellona, *alarmed for the safety of* Dennira, *flies to the Barracks and brings the General himself with a train of Warriors—Appearance of the General described—The combat rages with great fury—*Philothemis *takes off the General's wig and tramples it in the dust—*Dennira *seizes* Papinian's *wig and* claps it on the General's head—*Strange consequence of this manœuvre*—*Conduct of* Papinian *on the occasion*—*Chace interrupted by a stratagem of* Bellona—*Battle continues*—Crow-street *play-house in danger of being demolished*—*Distress of the Manager*—Apollo *interested for the Manager*—*Assumes the form of a musical Lord*—*takes his Violin*—*Plays an Adagio*—*Power of Music*—*Peace is restored*—*The Curtain rises and the Play begins.*

FIGURE AND FASHION;

OR

THE HEROINES.

THIRD CANTO.

OH might the bard some inspiration share,
From him who sung Belinda's ravished hair!
Oh might he borrow *Forteguerri's** verse,
And beauty's power and knightly deeds rehearse?
Or rival him, the banks of *Seine* along   †   5
Who told of Cleric feuds in lofty song,
The fatal Desk, that dire contention bred,
What hosts the Prelate and the Chanter led.
Attend, fair dames, and, courtly lovers, hear,
If martial scenes may captivate the ear.   10
Oh could the days of chivalry revive,
And champions bold to warring females give !
Then should the knights in listed fields decide
Claims of precedence—rival beauties pride—

* Author of *Ricciardetto*, a mock heroic poem.
† The *Lutrin* of *Boileau*.

And all the mighty questions, that perplex   15
With burning hearts the soft aspiring sex :
But flow'rs of chivalry no longer bloom ;
Or flourish only on the silent tomb.
The courteous knights are vanished from our ken,
In lounging days we live of little men.   20
What lady now may boast a courteous knight ?
What errant champions now for beauty fight ?
To whom shall dames their wounded pride impart ?
Who slights avenge, that agonize the heart ?
Election quarrels, or a cast at dice   25
Can rouse contending champions in a trice ;
But none, like true-born knights, will take the field
When injured females must precedence yield.
Our youth are all of courtesy bereft,
Our females all to fight their battles left.*   30
Their snow-white hands the pond'rous lance sustain,
Their shoes embroider'd tread th' embattl'd plain.
Yet some exceptions, with delighted mind,
Ev'n in degen'rate times the muse can find.

----

* *Ariosto*—O gran bonta de cavelieri antithe.—

Our females yet exhibit noble rage, 35
When cards and dice their anxious thoughts engage.
But haste we onwards. In my former lay,
The rival dames commenc'd their cruel fray.
This canto brings their combat to a close.—
Then let my weary *Pegasus* repose. 40
Pretensions high inflam'd each haughty mind ;
Thrice with *Dennira* had the Duchess dined ;
Philothemis recounts her noble race,
Her husband's merits and exalted place.
In force so match'd were never heroines yet, 45
Since *Bradamante* and *Marfisa* met.
The Box-keepers aghast their fury view,
And wisely cautious from the fight withdrew.
Three times *Philothemis* renew'd th' attack,
As oft *Dennira's* legion drove her back. 50
But wounded honour so the fair sustain'd,
She pierc'd the lines, the leader's station gain'd.
And thrice she strove to pull her from her seat,
But ev'n to raise her was no trifling feat.
Endow'd with strength and weight her place to
      hold, 55
The dame was cast in nature's solid mold.—

F

So, when contending parties vex a nation,
Sits firmly fix'd some broad administration.*
Panting she paus'd, and cast around her eyes,
A waiter with a bowl of tea she spies,   60
Fragrant the tepid steam arose, and bland ;
She caught the bev'rage from the bearer's hand ;
Full in *Dennira's* face the bowl she threw,
The tea meand'ring down her bosom flew.
On the smooth orbs the milky currents glide ;   65
Thus thaws bedew the snow-crown'd hillock's side.
So, when her ample breast a wet-nurse shows,
The milk spontaneous from the nipple flows,

* There are some vile, vulgar words adopted in modern
politics—*Budget* and *Broad-bottomed* administration—*Budget* is
borrowed from the avocation of a tinker : It supposes the
minister to be an itinerant hireling, who deals in the basest
metal, proposes more than he can do, and undertakes to stop
the chinks and cracks of the leaky state, ruinous and rusty as
an old kettle.—*Broad-bottomed* administration is a vile phrase,
it is meant to express an administration of weight, *pon-
dere fixa suo,* but it may be turned to denote one that
shews its a—, according to the passage in *Shakspeare* (Measure
for Measure) *Esc.* What's your name, master Tapster ?
Pom.—Pompey. *Esc.*—What else ? *Pom.*—Bum, sir. *Esc.*
—Troth and your bum is the greatest thing about you, so
that in the beastliest sense, you are *Pompey* the great.—No
bad description of a *broad-bottomed* administration.

The spouting streams confess the source within,

And balmy currents irrigate her skin. 70

Lest pointed fragments should offend the fair,

The bowl of china was, by *Venus'* care,

So guided, that it lodged upon her breast,*

And, as a shield, that orb of beauty prest.

Adorn'd and guarded see the fair appear, 75

Thus eastern dancers bosom-cases wear.

Astonish'd, not dismay'd, *Dennira* stood,

And soon she dried away the milky flood.

Sternly she frown'd, as when with rage possest,

She drove unbidden youngsters from the feast.† 80

The foe came open-mouthed with rage impell'd;

An half-sucked orange as *Dennira* held,

Large as a cannon ball, not quite so hard;

With stedfast courage and with sharp regard,

She marked the vantage, her artillery ply'd; 85

There, where the portals of her face stood wide,

* The reader will find a very luxurious description of the dancing girls in Abbe *Raynal's* book. The good Abbe sometimes indulged himself, like his brother philosopher *Darwin*, in a strain of grave philosophical pruriency. He is truly eloquent in the subject of their bosom cases.

† Alludes to a curious story of *Dennira's* ejecting certain beaus from a party.

Forceful she drove her instrument of death,*
And stopt at once her triumph and her breath.
Sputt'ring she fell, the Tipstaffs came in aid,
Sped their commission, and the fair convey'd   90
To safe retreat, with small remains of life ;
Then all her partizans desert the strife.—
And now *Dennira* had the triumph gain'd,
And firm possession of the box retain'd :
But *Themis* sorrowing, mark'd her fav'rite's fate,   95
And new assailants join the fierce debate.—
Drest like a Six-clerk to the Courts she flew,
And summoned to the fight a motley crew.
Masters, and barristers, attorneys came,
With meek solicitors, an humble name ;   100
Some flaunt in silks, and some in tatter'd rags;
Some were slight armed, and some with loaded bags.
Ev'n ermin'd sages came to join the fray,
Who spread her rule with delegated sway.—

* Instrument of death.—Let not this expression be thought
hyperbolical, when applied to an Orange.—We are told that
Anacreon was choaked by a much smaller substance, a grape
stone. The Poet has very properly adapted the weapons with
which his Ladies fought to the delicacy of the female frame.

Like the stout swimmer, puffing thro' the ball,105
The noble * *Eolist* obeys her call,
And as he vented forth each spell of wind,
He gave a piece and parcel of his mind.
Next smooth * * *, sly and sneering still,
Came, more for love of mischief than good will. 110
He cared not who might victory obtain,
And only wish'd that he himself should gain.
An Elephant in size, without dispute,
And ev'n in sense, a wise, half-reasoning brute,
Came solemn * * * *'s gigantic form and vast : 115
The very pavement labour'd as he past.
Then *G——*, in simple, plain exterior join'd :
With sordid cunning of a vulgar mind :
Mild as the north wind, civil as the bear,
Half in judicial robes was *Wormwood* there. 120
With surly pride his downcast eye-ball scowl,
In deep long notes he does not speak, but growl :
Oh may he soon be placed at *N—'s* side
And all his sweetness to his ear confide.

* Eolists, a sect of ancient philosophers, who dealt much in puffing and ventosity.—See Swift's Essay on the mechanical operation of the spirit.

† So *Pope*—Half-reasoning Elephant.

F 3

Among the foremost, summoned by the dame ;   125
The bellowing _B——_, for ever forward, came.
Not him I mean in equity profound,
But him more frequently in _Green-street_ found.
Of _Macs_ a pair I mark'd among the croud,
Elate in hope, of courtly favour proud.   130
At Levee too I mark'd them in the press,
With gay pretensions, splendid as their dress.
Oh just pretensions, happy is the wight,
That Princes can approach, or Farces write !
Grim as a collier, with precursive roar,   135
Foaming and sweating like a hunted boar,
Axungia came, and _B——_ was in his wake,
Yet reeking warm his vacant chair to take.*
There shall he shine another and the same,
With equal dignity and equal fame.   140
A dingy mist ascended as he went,
With flagging wings the breeze received the scent,
The ducklings quak'd, the sky was overcast,
The weather-glasses fell where'er he past.
He too was there, who double worth display'd, 145
In Chanc'ry solemn, martial on parade,

∽∽∽∽∽∽∽

* Alludes to some projected or rumoured judicial arrange-
ments in the Island of _Barataria._

By *Corney* singled from th' aspiring bar,
And master named for mastery in war.
With scowling brow pedantic ******* goes,
Hibernian *Garret*, fam'd for length of nose.   150
Sober and prim as any ancient maid,
The thrifty ***** marches to their aid.
They claim his presence in a double right,
Master by day, Policeman in the night.
Such promptitude must win *Papinian's* grace,   155
Too long repugnant to the sale of place.*
With cuffs of scarlet and with coat of blue,
Then prating *M*——— † waddled with the crew;
" Silence and order," *D*—— full oft exclaim'd,
But his and *N*———'s tongues would not be tam'd;
Ambitious stationer, on objects high   161
Of twofold kind he squints with leering eye;
To conservator's chair at once he looks,
And pompous *A*———'s shop and gilded books,
High-minded man, who scarce a nod affords   165
To commoners, and keeps his bow for lords.

———————

* I believe we should read *plaice* here, in allusion to some
obscure story about Fishmonger's contracts.

† He was peculiarly fit for the ranks of *Themis*, both as
having a shop in the Four Courts, and being a conservator.

With judgment like his voice both strong and clear,
Papinian takes his station in the rear;
The post of danger wisely he declined,
Good generals still in safety should we find. 170
All these and countless more to *Crow-street* throng,
Old *Liffey* wonders as they march along.

   Dennira needed to resist the crowd,
All strength and courage that her stars allow'd;
But heav'n, that always makes the brave its care,
Brought new assistance to sustain the fair.   176
Bellona mark'd the foe's approach from far,
And sought the General to support the war;
Her the slow cart-horse, and the scarlet cloak,
A private trooper of the guards bespoke.* 180
She trotted slowly, 'twas her swiftest rate,
And timely enter'd at the Barrack gate.
She called as shrill as cock announcing morn,
She called as loud as loudest bugle-horn.
" Turn out the picket, † and to *Crow-street* haste."
—She added not, but to *Kilmainham* past, 186

* The Dragoon Guards or Green Horse.

† The Picket guard, which is always ready against cases
of emergency.

The seat of war, and piety of yore,*
The Templar's cross when streaming banners bore;
Now invalids their frugal porridge eat,.
While gay *Dennira* spreads the sumptuous treat. 190
The general in the surgeon's hands she found,
On either shin appear'd a desp'rate wound ;†
While *R———y*, a *Machaon* in his art,
With fomentations sooth'd th' offended part:
The scars of honour on his front ~~appear~~, 195
Tho' foil'd in fight with ambush'd tubs of beer.‡
So, when *Achilles* war with *Xanthus* wag'd;
The splashing fight in foaming liquor rag'd.—
His wig uncurled with amber current swims,
A petticoat invests his mighty limbs ; 200
His small-cloaths in the conflict wet and torn,
Left his posteriors naked and forlorn.

‑‑‑‑‑‑‑

* *Kilmainham*, now an hospital for invalids, and also the residence of some general officer, was formerly a commandery of the Knights of St. *John* of *Jerusalem*.

† A famous army surgeon and member of the medical board and hospital staff, in the time of the *Trojan* war. See *Gazette d'Homere*.

‡ This alludes to an incident which actually took place at Mrs. *Peter's* collation.—The worthy General fell over some tubs of beer or porter and spoiled his uniform, particularly his small-cloaths.

In vain for galligaskins might he call,
Thy breeches, *Peter*, were by half too small.
That good *Petrina*, gentle as she's fair,   205
Wears not the breeches, let the muse declare.
An highlander you might the Gen'ral vote,
But dimity compos'd his petticoat.
Far happier function it perform'd of old,
Petrina's beauteous members to enfold ;   210
Now it conceals, puff'd out in high relief,
The great posteriors * of the valiant chief.
" Gen'ral arise, for this important now,
" Is fraught with ornaments to crown thy brow ;†
" To *Crow-street* haste, where laurels may be found ;
" And desp'rate foes thy better half surround."

Soon as the Goddess pour'd upon his ear 217
The dangers that await his dearest dear,
He stays not to prepare his good grey steed ;
(For soldiers double ride, in case of need;) 220

----

* Some copies read, " anterior," *Baudius Arsenius* prefers it,
and it is sanctioned by the *Toledo* manuscript ; I should therefore be inclined to let it stand in the text.

† " Ornaments to crown thy brow." That was calculated
to excite a variety of ideas, and applied equally to his hopes
of honour and his fears of disgrace. The abruptness of the
address has great energy and spirit.

On her alone his whole attention dwelt,
His trim forgotten and his wounds unfelt:
Behind *Bellona* on the crupper plac'd,
In martial mood this pair to *Crow-street* pac'd
Nor helm, nor hawberk, nor the shining brand
The warrior took—a truncheon arm'd his hand. 226
Thus, when *Albracea's* * beauteous maid they sought,
One steed with *Ferraü, Rinaldo* brought.

Now might the hostile troops each other view,
And mutual rancour at the prospect grew.   230
A pass from *Crow-street* leads to *Temple-bar,*
There light and heavy bands commence the war;
Unguarded this *Papinian* hop'd to find,
No 'vantage ever scap'd his wary mind; †
A soldier old, in senate and in field,   235
Well practis'd when to strike, and when to yield.
At this eventful time the Gen'ral came;
His presence fill'd his troops with warlike flame:

----

* *Angelica,* the daughter of *Galafron—*See *Orlando Furioso.—*
Book the first.

     " Non lascie a piedi il buon figliuol *d'Amone,*
     " Con prieghi invita, & al fin toglie in groppa,
     " Eper l'Orme *d'Angelica* galoppa."

† Questo *Brunel* si pratico e si astuto.

Against *Papinian* as he spurr'd his horse,
The pavement trembled with his solid course, 240
The mud of *Temple-bar* a vortex rose,
Then fell in sable torrents on his foes,
Papinian stepp'd aside, and 'scap'd unhurt,
But fat *M*—— was tumbled in the dirt.
As o'er some steepy bridge of single arch   245
The warriors o'er his mountain-belly march.
The waiters mark'd him as he groaning lay,
And to a chop-house bore the chief away. *

Now sober *D*—— the furious onset stay'd,
" Order, decorum, gentlemen," he said, †   250
" Ev'n in a battle let politeness reign."—
Then *N*—— chaunted forth an Orthian strain,
" Britons strike home "—The martial sound imparts
Redoubled energy to warlike hearts.

————

* Something is here omitted.—The author has not expressed himself clearly.   Quere; for what purpose Mr.
M—— was conveyed to the chop-house ? was it to eat, or to
be eaten ? I suspect the latter.—I have heard it whispered,
that his Calipash or Calipee were made into Turtle soup.

† The composed and dignified character of the judge, so
fond of order and decorum, so full of phlegm on every occasion, is well delineated here.

Dire was the fight with re-percussive shocks,255
Shoving and thrusting, furious blows and knocks.
The Deities among the crowd appear;
There *Themis* urg'd the fight, *Bellona* here.
But *Themis* ever should resistless sway;
Her bands to *Crow-street* cut their furious way.260
In lobby and in box was fight renew'd,
Porter and blood the valiant hands embrew'd.
Tea, coffee, negus, on the ground were spilt;
And warriors sunk, not wholly dead, but *kilt*.*
Unarm'd and naked fly the female bands;   265
The men pursue them, with rapacious hands.
We read in chronicles of ancient fame,
To *Roman* plays when *Sabine* ladies came,
On trembling dames impetuous warriors flew,
And every *Roman* blade his rapier drew.—   270
Oaths, shrieks, screams, scolding, groans, are heard
   afar,
The house presents a dreadful form of war,†

----

* An Hibernicism.—The combatants were not killed dead;
but destined to live a little longer, *more Hibernorum*.

    " ———— Crudelis ubique,
    " Luctus, ubique pavor, & plurima mortis
    " Imago."   VIRGIL.

† Fiat justitia, ruat cælum.
       G

Scratch'd faces, bloody noses, and crack'd crowns,

Torn waistcoats, tatter'd kerchiefs, wigs and gowns.

Such beauteous wigs as *Grecian* ladies drest,275

Such curls as flow'd o'er *Agrippina's* breast ;

Muffs, tippets, ruffs, and pads are scatter'd round;

Divorces, * purgatories, strew the ground ;

Beads, bugles, tassels, ribbands, fringes, lace,

Pennaches, turbans, hats are scatter'd through the

        place.   280

   As in the van the doughty Gen'ral stood,

Philothemis beheld in wrathful mood ;

She springs like light'ning to the foremost rank,

She smote his brows with steaming porter dank;

Then from his head the dripping wig she tore

And stamp'd contemptuous on the dusty floor;

And were it laurel it had been the same,   287

So full of fury was the warlike dame :

* *Divorces,* so called in the nomenclature of female dress, are certain articles or instruments, stiffened with iron and steel, which are applied to the Ladies breasts, to give them a proper degree of consistency and projection, by preventing their collapsing or coming too closely in contact with each other.— The *Purgatory* is a part of female dress, worn lower down.— Various conjectures may be formed as to the origin of the name.

Frowning he stood with head expos'd and bare;
To guard and grace it was *Dennira's* care.   290
But whence or how?—Lo where *Papinian* stands,
With waving curls that equity demands;
In swift reprisal, on the prey she flies;
And crowns her husband with the glorious' prize.
Not with more pride did chief of ancient *Rome*
In triumph bear the *opima spolia* home   296
Than did the Gen'ral.—As he past the crowd,
The tipstaffs to the wig official bow'd;
The mace the wig omnipotent obey'd;
The purse before him was in state display'd:300
The lawyers made obeisance as he went;
Th' attornies all in adoration bent.—
'Tis not the man that can attention call;
Symbols of pow'r, be sure, are all in all.
The crown, the sceptre, and the purple robe, 305
Will veneration claim around the globe.
Who cassoc short and sleeve of cambric wears,†
In God right reverend to the crowd appears.

* Let not the malicious reader take an improper meaning
from this line, as if the fair *Dennira* ever thought of adorning
or fortifying the brows of her husband in a manner contrary
to the Articles of War, with Hornworks, Halfmoons or the
like, introduced by French engineers.

† The habiliments of Episcopacy.

" Hark away, Tally ho"*—the stout *Papinian* cried,
All *Crow-street* rung and *Drury-lane* replied.   310
From ev'ry avenue the footmen bawl,
And orange-wenches scream from ev'ry stall;
The butchers dogs are heard with open throat,
And curs and turnspits join their treble note;
Carmen and porters, to partake the sport,   315
Mount their gall'd jades and gallop to the court.
The barristers and agents join the race;
Such hunting ne'er was seen since *Chevy Chace*.
Papinian † found his trusty hunter nigh,
He led the jolly train with potent cry.   320
O'er squeaking beldams in their haste they rode,
On sprawling pigs the fiery courser trode;
They splash'd, they dash'd, with frantic fear possest,
The mothers snatch'd their infants to the breast.‡

---

* This is highly in character.—*Papinian* who is a mighty
hunter before the Lord, has a view hollow of his wig breaking cover, and very properly pursues it in a grand style, as is
here described.

† The going off thus in the middle of the fight was a truly
politic stroke; this is what is called backing one's friends—as
Falstaff says.   This passage deserves to be studied, as containing a most excellent and instructive moral lesson.

‡ So V.rgil—" Et trepidæ matres presserunt ad ubera
natos."

The wise *Bellona* to divert the storm,   325
Drew off the hunters in a badger's form: *
Th' attractive scent the sportsmen keen pursue,
O'er the green hills, and vanish from the view.
The Gen'ral to the courts of justice went,
For to his brain the wig some crotchets lent;
His triumph o'er the foe seem'd incomplete, 331
If to the wig he added not the seat.
Some plodding lawyers at their briefs had stay'd,
They read, and wondered why the court delay'd;
They made obeisance when the wig they saw,
The Gen'ral sate and gave them martial law;
Then bade the Master-adjutant report,   337
And so *manœuvred* fairly out of court.

Meantime, without the play-house, and within,
The storm of battle raged with frightful din. 340
Tho' many from th' embattled field retir'd,
Those who remain'd, with double fury fir'd,
Bit, scratch'd, and tore.—their shouts spread far and
        wide
And what their numbers lost their rage supplied.

* Observe here a dignus vindice nodus, To make the triumph of her favorite complete *Bellona* contrives to draw off the hunters,

The heat of warring factions to compose,   345
The lovely Duchess from her seat arose,
With looks and accents that might well controul
The wild disorder of a maniac's soul.
" Now ken you weel, (the bonny Duchess cries)
" These cheels wull mak a muckle din arise.350
" What gars them thrang to sic envenom'd fra?
" Ca' the poleese and let them gang awa;
" Fou sair it makes me greet, 'tis unco strange
" Sae wild disorder thrae the hoose shad range."

In vain her Grace this eloquence bestow'd ;355
Still, still they roar'd, and still the combat glow'd ;
And such the furious appetite for fight,
The play-house had been sack'd that very night
Had not *Apollo* heard in gentle tones
The rising orisons of pious *Jones.*   360
Not with more piety or more despair,
To father *Jove, Eneas* breath'd his prayer, *
When *Trojan* matrons, urg'd by *Juno's* ire,
Or potent stingo, set his ships on fire:
In *A———'s* shape the God from heaven descends;
Athwart his breast the ribband blue extends ;366

* See Eneid, Book 5th Line 685.
    " Tum pius Eneas humeris obscindere vestem," &c.

His florid hue and simp'ring face he wore,
A brisky juvenile, not quite fourscore.*
He held the fiddle, and the bow he ply'd;
Like L———h, *Mercury* was at his side;   370
And sooty *Vulcan* with a limping pace,
Behind them carried an enormous bass.

  Oh power of music! savage is the breast,
That has not concord of sweet sounds confest?
" Hush ev'ry breeze" th' immortal fiddler play'd;
The din subsided, and the fight was stay'd.   376
A sweet *Adagio* to the tune succeeds,
A tender strain, that melancholy feeds,
Then, *Siciliano*, innocent and kind,
To mutual fondness sooth'd the hostile mind. 380
The warriors to the ground their weapons threw,
To clasp each other in embrace they flew;
By mutual aid they recompose their hair,
And all disorders of their dress repair.
Those who so late were interchanging blows, 385
Sate amicable now, in peaceful rows:
Discord was dumb and Emulation dead,
All contests now, but of politeness fled.

———————

* Apollo was endowed with perpetual youth, vid. Pantheon.

Philothemis the box disputed gain'd,
The next *Demira* quietly retain'd;   390
And all the rest without a murmur sate
As *Macanally* pleas'd, or ruling fate.
The curtain rose—the silence was profound.
Thus harmony the power of music crown'd.*

✻ Thus happily ended this great contest for the present;
but as the ladies are so apt to put themselves into heats, I
would advise, in order to keep them cool, that to the present
refreshments at the drawing-rooms of the Duchess. such as
lemonade, orangeade, and orgeat, ices may be added.

THE

AMAZONIAD;

OR,

Figure and Fashion:

AN

HEROIC POEM.

PART THE SECOND,

CONTAINING

CANTOS THE FOURTH AND FIFTH,

COMPRIZING

Characters and Anecdotes wholly new.

━━━━━━

Ecce iterum Crispinus !
Ha !—art thou there, old Truepenny.

━━━●●●●⟨⟪⟫⟩●●●●━━━

Dublin:

PRINTED BY JOHN KING,
No. 2, Westmorland-street.

▬▬

1806.

TO THE READER.

COURTEOUS Reader, (for thy fair reception of the former part justly entitles thee to that appellation) I am sensible of thy kindness, and feel that I cannot better return it, than by continuing my labours and lucubrations for thine emolument and delight, and for the reformation of the world, in general. I here present thee, therefore, with a second crop or gathering, of the fruits of my diligent enquiries ; and indefatigable researches, but allow me, my very good friend, to caution thee against two things.—First, against an over eager desire to be acquainted with my name and person,—it will only produce trouble to me, and disappointment to thee ; for be assured, it is a desire, which neither can, nor shall be gratified. The learned author of *Pursuits of Literature* was not more studious

B

of concealment, nor did he take more effectual
measures to secure himself, from discovery,
than I have done. Living or dying, let me
swim or sink, as *George Falkner's* wife said,
I will retain possession of my secret. Beware,
therefore, of indulging thyself in guesses,
and conjectures, on this subject, and publishing, in all the pride of self-sufficient sagacity,—" That you know,—that you could tell
" if you chose the name of the author—that
" it begins with an A, or a B, or a C, or
" any other letter of the alphabet.—That he
" lives not an hundred miles from a certain
" street or square—that he lodges in a ground
" floor or in a garret." All this is the cant
of persons who affect to know more—than
they really do. There are at least four and
twenty poets, all on record in *Dublin*, any
one of whom would be fully competent to
write the poetry of these productions, though
not any of them, perhaps, or all of them put
together, might be able to acquire and retain
the various information they convey. By
guessing any of the live poets, of the present

age and country, thou wouldst pay the person
a compliment, but mightest do him a disser-
vice. Thou mightest be the officious cause
of depriving him of sundry gracious nods,
familiar salutes, and condescending winks,
smiles, grins, and shakes by the hand, from
various persons, consequential, and of consequence—noble, and ennobled ; and of sundry
dinners from lord mayors, sheriffs, aldermen,
wine merchants, church dignitaries.—Idle
conjectures of this kind may sow the seeds of
discord through a whole town, and make the
most intimate friends and acquaintances look
glum on each other. I would not wish on
the one hand, to be defrauded of the reputation, whatever it may be, attending the author of these productions ; nor on the other,
would I wish, that any honest gentleman
should be pressed into the service, and obliged
to father opinions and sentiments of which he
disapproves,—to reprobate his most intimate
friends, and to praise those he dislikes. Let
me enjoy undisturbed my anonymous fame—
the consciousness of doing good, by stealth,

and improving the world, without fee or reward, and let me go to the grave in silence
and secrecy.

Another piece of advice let me give thee,
my loving and much respected friend. Do
not be too confident in thine own sagacity,
or too desirous of exhibiting it to the world,
by filling up the blanks or expounding the
asterisks in this work of mine. If thou hast
any conscience, thou wilt reflect that every
author, if known, must be answerable to the
world—if concealed, must be answerable to
the tribunal of his own conscience, and to
Heaven, both for his work and the consequences of it.   By the extension of this rule
I shall be made answerable, not only for what
is really, but for what is apparently mine.
Thus shall I be made responsible for thy erroneous guesses, whether that error proceeds
from stupidity or malice.   Many will be found
who, from ignorance of the town, and stupidity, kindred to thy own, may take all thy
guesses for gospel, and impute to the nameless author, absurdities which are all thy own.

Thus, when I am speaking of the public executioner with his cat o'nine tails, if thou shouldst say I mean a member of the legislature, whether lord or commoner—when I talk of a banker's clerk, if thou shouldst say I mean a chancellor of the exchequer—when I speak of a church dignitary, if thou shouldst say I mean a captain of dragoons—when I talk of an old woman, if thou shouldst say I mean a general officer.—All these eccentric guesses and conjectures of thee, O, reader! thou seest, will be laid at my door, as if I had really meant the personages whom thou art pleased to designate. I have frequently attended in a corner of a bookseller's shop, since the publication of my poem, and heard, with no small astonishment, some self-sufficient coxcomb, with great volubility, expounding to a gaping auditory all the mysteries which had cost me so much time. This is a great vanity and sore trouble under the sun.—" Why " should I (thought I within myself as I lis- " tened) why should I have taken all this " pains, and dried my brains like the roe of

" a red herring with watching, and study, and
" raking, and wenching, all for the edificati-
" on of the world, to meet such a vexatious
" return ? Let my readers amuse themselves
" on a Sunday evening, with reading over
" my learned poem, and guessing at the enig-
" mas it contains ; it is pleasant and harm-
" less, but let them not presume, to be as
" wise as the author; and publish to all the
" world pretended keys, which are supposed
" to unlock the secret recesses and nests of
" drawers of his escritoir." Often was I
tempted, to consign these two last and favourite cantos to the flames, or some meaner
destiny ; but fate, and some lurking portion
of literary *storgè* or paternal fondness restrain-
ed my hand. So I determined to give my
writings to the devil—and as the devil would
have it, and through his diligent ministry, they
are presented unto thee, O courteous reader !
Enjoy the gift, and thank the donor for his
bounty. Remember the fable of *Cupid* and
Psyche. It has a fine moral, which applies

to thee and me. The very moment I find
thee swayed by a foolish curiosity, and too
importunate, to see my face, and discover
my quality, our correspondence must end,
and I vanish from thee, never more to return.

AMAZONIAD ;

OR,

FIGURE AND FASHION.

SECOND PART.

CANTO IV.

BEING A CONTINUATION OF PART I.

ARGUMENT.

*INVOCATION—The Poet's desire of fame—The
Action is resumed—Indignation of* Eris, *or* Discord, *at
the cessation of hostilities between the belligerent powers
—The means chosen by her to revive the contention—
Strong claims of* Discord *on the Irish Government—
She repairs to the* Castle-spectre, *demands performance
of an Union-promise—He feels the justice of her claims
—Finds her booked for some favour, and resolves to
gratify her—For the purpose of procuring a scuffle, he
determines, as the most effectual means, to give a general Fete Champetre—Indiscriminate invitation of guests*

—*Some of the parties mentioned*—*Homeric catalogue*
—*Short account of the* Dejeuner,—*Emperor of* China
—*Doctor and his noble friend, a pair of ponies well
matched*—*A fat and comely lady well known*—*Great
eating*—*Great jollification*—Apollo *endeavours to preserve harmony, but in vain*—*Ill humours break out*—
The battle begins—*A desperate uproar*—*The Lobster*—
A new simile for the Lobster—*Different persons form
designs on the Lobster*—*Eloquent speeches*—*Of a learned Lord*—*of a famous Equity Pleader*—*Polite Conversation of the* Doctor *and* Axungia—Axungia *possesses
himself of the Lobster*—*Discomfiture of* Axungia—
Episode of two Right Reverends—*They quarrel.*

AMAZONIAD;

OR,

FIGURE AND FASHION.

FOURTH CANTO.

Yᴇᴛ once again, enamour'd of the theme,
I seek the martial dames near Liffey's stream;
I hail the military pomp from far,
The waving plumes, and dazzling files of war.
Heroic Amazons, the combat wage!   5
And let your Bard partake the noble rage.
Her Grace will plaudits to the strain allow;
And courtly W------n his mitre bow.
R--n--h shall praise; and all the Castle train
Cry—" Bravo, bravo: let him sing again."   10

Dear to the poet is the voice of Praise;
It throws a sun-shine o'er his wintry days;
It steals him from the nameless ills of life,
The duns importunate—the scolding wife;
It bids him at his betters curl his nose;   15
While Admiration whispers—" there he goes!"
If great the suff'ring, great is the reward
That waits the fasts and vigils of the Bard

The glorious palm of deathless song be mine,
And Pipes and Bishoprics I can resign;*   20
Untir'd I sing.—I feel the tuneful sport
Can make the weary path of Being short.
The work I plan, the monument design,†
Doom'd to survive this flitting form of mine.
The great Extinguisher of Time ere long   25
Must quench the Bard, and subjects of his song:
But Phœbus whispers, that my lofty rhymes
Shall please the Belles and Beaux of distant times.

The Muse in fancy had composed the strife:
But vain and fleeting are the hopes of life.   30
Arungia hop'd—but now he mourns in sprite,
The furs bestow'd on *Wormwood* the polite.
Discord with anguish from the scene retir'd,
She saw the truce with indignation fir'd.

" Shall I, in daily broils and faction nurst,   35
" Be stunn'd with harmony, with concord curst!
" In Church and Senate have I kindl'd war,
" Yet fail with women and the brawling bar!

------

* This seems an odd association of ideas.—Was a piper,
or a piper's son, ever made a bishop.

† Exegi Monumentum Ære-perennius.

" Who for promotion shall on me attend,

" With off'rings feed, or at my altars bend! **40**

" 'Tis told in Scripture, and by bards 'tis sung,

" What direful ills have from an apple sprung.

" Pernicious gift! an apple could deceive

" Contending goddesses, and mother Eve.

" Now, to th' occasion I the measure suit, **45**

" And tempt these females with a meal of fruit.

" The Castle-Spectre to my aid I call,

" This vaunted Union* shall to discord fall."

Nor was she slow the Spectre's lodge to find,

And glorious mischief brooded in her mind. **50**

The doors flew open, onward as she prest,

The paly phantom eager she addrest.

" The worth of *Discord* well to thee is known,

" The boasted Union—is it not my own?

" DIVIDE and GOVERN was the maxim still.— **55**

" I shap'd your measures with informing skill.

------

* Meaning only of the contending parties, mentioned in the former Cantos; not insinuating that the legislative *Union* between *England* and *Ireland* is likely to end in discord.

.C

" Pow'rless and vain had prov'd, without my aid,
" What lawyers scribbled,* what old *Corney* paid.†
" I taught the zealots of the Church to roar;
" I dy'd the zealots of the Cross in gore.   60
" I party Symbols gave, and party Names,
" And fill'd fraternal hearts with *stygian* flames.
" For such deserts, I should to thee be dear;
" For such deserts, be to the Palace near.—
" Of *Momus* now I shall become the sport.   65
" A truce inglorious chases me from Court.
" O shame! confusion! never be it said,
" That Discord fail'd where British counsels sway'd!
" Convoke th' attendant Belles and Beaux from far,
" Mine be it—to disperse the seeds of war."   70

Nor did she speak to inattentive ears.—
Her aid his friends had prov'd in former years.
Her recent Union services he own'd:
And Union-promises have all been crown'd.—
He plann'd a breakfast; sent his cards abroad;   75
Full fifty porters sweated with the load.
O glorious rout, that cause of Discord prov'd,
Such *Dejeuner*, as ancient chaos lov'd!

* A multitude of Union pamphlets by Judges and Barristers,
† To members whose TERMS were—CASH!

He wish'd to palliate, he might not recal
The doom severe, that thinn'd St. *Patrick's* hall. 80
All hues of party in the list were seen—
Red, white, and Orange, purple, blue, and Green.*
Sects various, as the party-colour'd hues,
Churchmen, and Romanists, with Turks and Jews.
For much delight he felt, or chose to feign, 85
To see the general Saturnalia reign.
Gamblers and Statesmen, Churchmen, men of Law;—
No Lord-May'r's feast a greater medly saw.
United Brethren posted to the board.
And Orange Lodges rush'd, a furious horde. 90
Moravians, Swaddlers, Anabaptists came;
A Walker walk'd, a non-descript of fame.

Discord delighted, hail'd the motley crew,
More pied assemblage never charm'd her view.
The proud encampment rose, the streamers play, 95
Bright as the pheasant's plume, or popinjay.
Near crowded *Cairo* thus, of various dies,
And various forms, the proud pavillions rise:

* The effects of certain colours on the organs of certain
animals is truly surprising. We know what paroxysms scarlet
excites in the turkey-cock; certain brutes are equally annoyed
by the colour—Green.

To *Mecca* when the pilgrim train repair,
Intent to mingle merchandize and pray'r.   100
The feast was suited to the public taste ;
Ten thousand cates in jellies and in paste.
Earth, water, air, to crown the board purvey'd ;
Apicius never such a treat display'd.
Each fam'd alembic, and each noblest vine,   105
Combin'd to furnish the liqueurs and wine.
But what distinguish'd most the sumptuous *fete,*
The master look'd as if he never ate.

Methinks, in *Lucian,** I have read at school,
For *Hecate* how suppers were kept cool.   110
If suppers waited thus the queen of hell,
A ghost might sure a breakfast give as well,
Some, who such ghostly converse ill enjoy,
Might well a spoon of double length employ.†
So well the cook and *traiteur*‡ play'd their part, 115
That all the produce seem'd of magic art.

* Εχαίης Δεισνοι This was a very public kind of entertainment, being usually laid out at a place where three roads met.

† Alluding to the foolish old proverb, " He who eats
with the Devil must have a long spoon."

‡ Beware, reader, not to read this word amiss—*Traiter.*
It is a French word, and means a furnisher of entertainments.
By a false pronunciation you might make me say that
traiters were employed at the secretary's breakfast.

There gourmandize exults by science taught,
And distant climates were together brought.
And, ranz'd in order, at the board we find,
Thy caviar, *Moscow*, with the spice of Ind.   120
Along the board had *Y - - - - s* employed his skill,
Near every cover was a gilded pill,
Soap of Castile and Calomel combin'd,
From bile the bowels free, from grief the mind,

All that the muses have rehears'd before   125
Were there conven'd, and countless myriads more.
Chief in the train our eyes a couple strike
Alike in principles, in wigs* alike,
Fierce in polemics, and of zeal untain'd,
In person squat, but for politeness fam'd,   130
As arm in arm they came, loquacious, bland,
One coil'd a clew of packthread round his hand.
And much he talk'd with deep discerning look
Of Councils, Fathers, and Sir *Edward Cook.*

- - - - - - -

* Wigs —The near connexion between wigs and the principles which fill the head of the wearer, has been already noticed by *Pope* in these lines:

    " A joke on *Jekyll*, or some odd old Whig,
    " Who never changes principles or wig."

Like ponies match'd a curricle to draw,   135
*Eblana's** double pontiff there I saw.
Alike their stature, and alike their port,
They pace the streets, and haunt the viceroy's
          court,
The stunted twins, of mother church in age,
Their busy heads intrigues of state engage.   140
That they are two, by sportive Chance was done,
For Nature had design'd to make them one :
And Chance, to consummate the jadish trick,
Gave one to *Paddy*, † one to *Dominick*.
There too, of young divines I mark'd a croud, 145
Unheard in pulpits, at a fox chase loud.
To doxies they in the Bordellos preach,
Or newest creeds of boots and breeches teach.
Yet mitres strangely on such heads may light.
By means inscrutable to human sight.   150

A lady there appeared of comely port,
Ere while an ornament of *Rutland's* court.

＊＊＊＊＊＊

* The classical name for the city of *Dublin*.

† Made Paddy D. vicegerent of the one—made the other
a *Dominican* friar. They are short and zealous, though un-
lovely in their lives ; in their deaths they should not be
divided.

She look'd thro' manhood with sagacious ken,
Experienc'd judge of measures and of men.
Tho' vig'rous sage, and mellow ripe, tho' fresh, 155
And fat, * as if she fed on human flesh.
Forward she push'd her daughters, train'd with art,
In active life to take the manly part.
Papinian, stationed at the phantom's side,
Prepar'd the loaves and fishes to divide. 160
Chief Justice Joker, with some jovial souls,
Snug in a corner took his butter'd rolls,
And *Mac* —— in his birth day pride,†
Fine as a daw, was at his comrade's side.
There *China's* emperor, with a courtly air, 165
Grimace important, and a vacant stare,
And motion, as if made of brittle ware,

* This may surprize the reader, at first glance; but
flesh to flesh is a natural principle of production and encrease.
All systems of organized matter naturally coalesce with their
like; it is therefore reasonable to presume that human flesh
should be nutritious food to human creatures: and that a
lady who has her belly full of it will be apt to encrease in
size.

† This gentleman was a conspicuous figure at the last
birth day levee. The old Castle stagers were astonished at
the apparition.

Advancing sate, with a peculiar grace,
Where rank and fashion filled the foremost place.
Cares of politeness all his thoughts employ,   170
His bottle he produc'd—dispens'd his soy.
The fan he spreads, the gentle labour plies,
To guard the ladies from intruding flies.

In varied mirth the sportive moments roll'd,
Some laugh'd, some sung, and others bargains sold :
The point of converse fashion loves to hit,   176
Where ribbald grossness bears the palm of wit.
The ladies eat and drink, and drink again,
While copious draughts of perfect love they drain,
And as the cups of nectar circled round,   180
The potent fumes their upper regions found.

A peal of laughter sounded from afar,
It seem'd the crash of elemental war ;
So shrill, so harsh, that never did I hear
A burst of mirth so painful to an ear.   185
Oh ! 'twas a Doctor, * loudest of the loud,
Or in the mirthful, or the brawling croud.

———

* Quere. What Doctor ?—I presume some physician.
The author seems partial to the profession. It cannot be
Doctor *Plunket*. He is rather sly and sardonic than noisy.

A mingled clamour from the camp arose,
While with the circling glass the clamour grows.
Perplex'd attention thousand tongues divide,   190
A thousand sounds are wafted far and wide,
The glasses, salvers, and decanters ring.—
Some lead the dance, and some prepare to sing.
The martial ministrels, station'd on the plain,
Alternate wak'd the spirit-stirring strain.   195
The prescient God of harmony and day,
Perceiv'd what lurking seeds of mischief lay.
Again he tried, if concord of sweet sound
Might banish discord from the chosen ground,
In vain the God essays his tuneful pow'r,   200
Fell Discord waits to seize th' appropriate hour.

'Tis come, 'tis come : what shrieks resound from
          far,
What *Stygian* trumpet brays the note of war.
Death and damnation ! fury and despair !
Cries, groans and hisses fill the troubled air,   205
Sobs, wailings, weepings, menace, martial clang,
Envenom'd stab, reiterated bang.
The clarion shrill, the bagpipe's drowsy hum,
The dull incitement of the double drum.
The bugle horn—the hautboys varied breath,   210

Resound a prelude to the dance of death.—
Come on, *Bellona*, mingle in the roar.
Come, all ye Furies, lap your fill of gore,
Tables were overthrown and jars o'erturn'd,
And leaves of gooseberries were in porter churn'd.
As caution guided, or adventrous rage,   216
Some darts employ—some hand to hand engage.
With brandy, and the rage of combat warm'd,
Some brandish'd knives, and some with forks were
          arm'd.
Gnaw'd pippins, orange skins, and bones they threw;
Like patt'ring hail the show'rs of walnuts flew. 221
The *Battle* of the *Boxes* was a fray
Of cranes and pigmies, to this dreadful day;
Plates, dishes, jugs, decanters, glasses hurl'd,
It seem'd the last convulsion of the world.   225
The sky was darken'd with the missile storms,
And slaughter wore ten thousand hideous forms.
Oh! have you seen by skilful artist wrought,
How valiant *Laphitha* with centaurs fought?*
How some carous'd, and some the foe assail'd, 230
And death and riot thro' the scene prevail'd?

* See Ovid. Metamorph. book 12th, at the nuptials of
Piritheus and *Hippodamia.*

The horses startled at the horrid sound :
Cars, Chariots, Berlins roll'd promiscuous round.

Say, Muses, whence the dire confusion came.
Two causes chief awak'd the murd'rous flame. 235

A giant Lobster fill'd a mighty dish.
From *Saltees** never came so vast a fish.
Long had the tyrant rul'd with griping claw,
And ship-wreck'd sailors fill'd his ample maw.—
So, when some prelate yields to feasts and fate, 240
With purple pall the monster lies in state,
Preserving ev'n in death the priestly red,
Doom'd to feed others who so largely fed.—
Majestic Lobster! how the *Doctor* gloats !
Thy tail *Arungia* to his paunch devotes.— 245
C - - - side-long view'd thee with enamour'd eye :
But could not bear to leave a partridge-pye.
With truffles fill'd, the viand came from far :
He seiz'd it, as a contraband of war.
C - - - - - l the fish in right of kindred claim'd, 250
Whose ample face with hue congenial flam'd :

＊＊＊＊＊＊

† Saltees are islands near the coast in the county of Wexford, from whence great store of Lobsters is sent to *Dublin*.

But near *Madeira* she so long delay'd,
Her tott'ring legs th' incumbent weight betray'd.
The Cape she visited, she eame to Port,
But tumblers of Madeira were her forte.   255

All eloquent began the Lord of Law;
And twin'd the packthread, as he wagg'd his jaw.—
" Who claims this fish, this monster of the main ?
" It is a deodand, I will maintain.
" If *Flotsam jetsam ligan* it was taken,   260
" 'Tis droit of Admiralty, I find in *Bacon.*
" I've search'd for precedents :—in *Styles* we read,
" Who lobsters dress, to crack the claws proceed.
" But then, on principle, it must appear,
" The task belongs to any person here.—   265
" I have a manuscript of Serjeant *Bish,*
" Reports from *Billingsgate,* and title *Fish.*—
" On Midland Circuit,—no, it was the Home.—
" A case of Lobsters did to trial come.—
" The point was sav'd, by Lord Chief Justice *Ryder.*
" But, apropos ! I hate your Irish Cyder,   271
" Too much of apple flavour it retains."
Here - - - - - - - - bellow'd out indignant strains.—*

* Observe here some fine touches of nature, and beautiful
delineations of character. The manly - - - - - - - listens,

So loud the scolding tones, they might derange 265.
An hundred fish-women, at Oyster-change.*

But now a figure bolted from the crew,
In form diminutive, in face a Jew.—
Such as he was, he flourish'd in his day ;
And led the files of war in proud array. 270
His oratory seem'd almost the moan
Of those who cry " Cast Clothes" in plaintive tone,
" In truth, my lord, and greatest verity,
" No principle to meet the case I see.
" Before we dress the fish, or touch a claw, 275
" Consult the judges, learned in the law.
" Or let the proper officer report,
" Meantime, the lobster may be lodged in court.
" With humble deference I do insist— —"
A doctor† fell'd him with his brawny fist. 280

with much patience, to the law arguments of his noble friend ,
but when he comes to asperse the character of Irish cyder,
the patriotic feelings of the honest gentleman flame out,
and he bellows with a becoming indignation.

* I know no such place in *Dublin.* Edit.

† The impatient character of the redoubtable doctor alluded to, is well preserved here. It is a pity he interrupted
the prosing discourse of the sober orator.

D

It chanc'd one impulse to one spot should lead
Two chiefs, who seldom in their views agreed,
From different parts the rival doctors came,
Axungia's stronger arm enforc'd his claim.
With chairman's action should'ring to the dish,   285
He stretch'd his mutton paw—he grasp'd the fish.
He grinn'd with pleasure—stript the coat of mail,
And to his ample chops applied the tail.
Grim as the Cyclops, in old *Homer's* song,
When one he seis'd among the *Grecian* throng,   290
The body to his spacious mouth applied,
And crack'd the bones, and suck'd the vital tide.
The *Doctor* saw in wrath, and ireful mood,
Churchman profest, but Romanist in blood.
Oh ! have you heard the loud tremendous roar ?   295
When rustics ring the snout of sturdy boar.*
" Did ever scoundrel gobble in such haste,†
" A popish thief !—on lobsters he must fast !
" On Fridays, when I spy a fellow feeding,
" I quickly trace his principles, and breeding.   300
" He in his belly has the Pope of *Rome*,
" Rebels and Papists all from *Wexford* come,—

* This line is a beautiful example of alliteration.
† This is just specimen of *D* . . . .'s manner.

" That rascal much mistakes my loyal mind,
" Who thinks to eat the lobster I design'd—
" I meant to put him in the *Bishop's Court*,   305
" A dang'rous recusant, of *Popish* sort."

Arungia, foaming, rush'd inflam'd with ire,
His upper end smoak'd like a house on fire.
Exuding poison of a toad or asp,
The lobster yet remain'd within his grasp.   310
Pond'rous and large and thorny were the claws,
The doctor smote the doctor on the jaws.
Clatt'ring the weapon fell, like pond'rous mace.—
All arm'd in leather was the doctor's face :
Yet, punctures sore projecting thorns imprest,   315
And spouting blood bedew'd his sturdy breast.
Not unreveng'd—a vase both large and sweet,
Of bronze stood near, for ladies' uses meet.
Nor had this useful vessel stood forlorn,
The fair had oft replenish'd it, that morn.   320
'Tis strange how ladies will agree in that,
At other points, in contradiction flat !
Such with our rival heroines was the case,
That very morn they both enjoy'd the vase.
But, as the bard was not allow'd to look,   325
He cannot tell you which precedence took.

D 2

This much in ancient records may be read,
Their contributions bath'd *Arungia's* head.
The doctor heav'd—he turn'd it upside down;
O'erwhelm'd with spray, his rival bears the crown;
With equal grace, though not so plump, of yore, 331
La Mancha's knight *Mambrino's* helmet wore.
As boots or cloth, that water-proof are held,
A greasy face the gushing streams repell'd,
In copious rills a tide of amber flow'd,   335
The vase above, a crown pontific shew'd.—
With brow of menace came a chieftain hoar,
And from the field his baffled brother bore.—

While thus they rag'd, with dismal din and loud,
Two mitred veterans met amid the croud.   340
As creeps the wily fox, with looks askance,
When some fat goose allures an am'rous glance ;
Bold, yet suspicious, rolls his felon eyes,
Keen for advantage, fearful of surprise.—
As, when the venal fair at close of day,   345
To seek adventures takes her devious way,
Her reconnoitring eyes incessant rove,
To catch the votary of wine and love.—
As in confessional the friar leers,
When, towards his box some tempting damsel steers.
So leer'd *O'* - - - - - -, while *M*—— seem'd to show 351
Half buck, half priest, half *Pre* - - - *e* and half beau.

Smooth as his shaven chin, his port appears,
Smooth as the silk, he in his cassock wears.
For who, like him, by flatt'ry could prevail? 355
Who messages convey, or bear a tale?
Yet supple to the great, and crouching low,
He to the little, decent pride could show.

They met—they paus'd—in silent wonder gaz'd
Each at his brother's goodly trim amaz'd. 360
And first, *O'B* - - - - - " What, thou a B - - - - p" cries,
" What, thou a B - - - - p," *W* - - - - - - - - replies.—
" Thou, from *Parisian* cloisters wear the lawn!"
" And thou from a collector's office drawn!"

" Let us not mingle in the martial ring: 365
" But watch the chance that may translation bring.
" Fierce thro' the combat let archbishops range,
" While we confer, and friendly gifts exchange."*

* This meeting and familiar conference in the midst of a
battle is perfectly *Homeric*. The reader, who is generally
fond of indulging his ingenuity, at the expence of an author's
reputation will perhaps endeavour to apply what is mere
fiction, and the creation of the poet's brain, to some living
characters, with whom the author is in habits of great inti-
macy, and for whom he feels the utmost reverence. But if
he should, the fault is in the reader, not the writer, and
my highly exalted, and much respected friends will know
how to put the saddle on the right horse.

They sought a neighb'ring thicket, hand in hand,
And *W* - - - - - - - - - began, with aspect bland. 370

" Say, by what arts, the courtly game was play'd,
" That bids us meet in Fortune's masquerade ?"

" No common merits (said *O'B* - - - - -) were mine,
" By nature form'd in politics to shine.
" And cultivated, by a Jesuit's care,   375
" To turn to profit her endowments rare.
" In daily Journals paragraphs to write;
" A pamphlet pen, or an address indïte ;
" By whispers to cement or break a league,
" And oil the hinges of some dark intrigue." 380

" In public toils, if you (said *M* - - - - -) shine;*
" Domestic services I claim as mine :
" My solid merits patriots will allow —
" *Venus* and *Mars* high-priesthoods can bestow.

- - - - - - -

* *Interdum bonus domitat Homerus.*—The author's memory
seems here to have been somewhat treacherous ; a few lines
before he calls one of his interlocutors *W* - - - - - - - -, and
now, behold he terms him *M* - - - - - : verily, master poet
here is a slip of the pen. But liars, they say, have need of
good memories.   ARISTARCHUS.

" Great ones, like children, pap and sugar need :—
" No common art their appetite can feed. 386
" Each wincing great one has some private sore :
" No common art can touch that tender core. *
" Nor is the knowledge granted to the crowd,
" To cringe in season, timely to be proud. 390
" Let this suffice.—Hark, in your private ear—
" But do we not descry old *D* - - - - - here ?
" Say, should he fall amid the hostile press,
" What child of Fortune shall his spoils possess ?"
" Mine, (said *O'B* - - - - -) if seniors may prevail." 395
" Mine, (*M* - - - - - cry'd) if vigour turns the scale."

This cause of strife embroil'd the loving friends.†
Eris, unseen, to fan the flame attends,
Like rival cats they rag'd, like troopers swore.
They bit, they scratch'd, they pummell'd, and they
tore.— 400
Their beavers large were trampled on the ground.
Their powder'd curls were scatter'd piece-meal
round.

* " Cui male si palpere recalcitrat undique tutus."
HORACE.

† This passage gives an admirable picture of human life
and contains an excellent moral lesson. The friendships of
courtiers are fleeting and transitory indeed.

Their silken cassocs past in shreds away:
And ev'n their small-clothes vanish'd in the fray.
Like *Sans-Culottes*,* they rag'd in direful mood. 405
And now their desperate claws were dy'd in blood,
The hue appropriate to their rank supplied,
And streams empurpled each right reverend hide.
Like wights, whom larceny compels to strip,
Or novices beneath monastic whip.   410
Or as *John Bull*, to buy heroic deeds,
At ev'ry vein his life-blood money bleeds.

Two hungry mastiffs join their furious rage,
And mortal combat for a pullet wage.
Two swine obscene advance with piercing cries, 415
In sturdy conflict, for less noble prize.
The savage multitude—the waggish boys,
Enjoy the triple fight, with mingled noise.

----

* *Sans Culottes.*—This comparison not only illustrates the
appearance of the combatants, divested of a certain superfluity
of dress, but also the rage, with which they were inspired,
resembling that which possest the Parisian mob, or Sans-Culottes, as they affected to call themselves. The author might
also wish to intimate, that his reverend champions had attained
to eminence on the principles of Sans-Culotterie, the rule and
principle of which has ever been to abase the Castle and the
Palace, and exalt the pig-sty and the dung-hill. I vow to
Jupiter I mean no personal allusion.

The two-legg'd combatants are overthrown,
And scarce the human from the brute is known ; 420
So bruis'd to mummy, so transform'd with ire,
So painted, so disguised with gore and mire.
Pigs, dogs, and *Pr - - - - s*, roll'd in dust and blood,
In social discord scramble to the flood.—
Old *Liffey* opes his arms, and on his breast, 425
With froth and offals wafts them from the feast.—
But let me not attend them on their way ;
Lest I, perhaps, beyond my depth should stray.
What life-boat then might save the bard from death?
What apparatus could restore his breath ? 430
Here will he pause, nor venture from the shore,
Ere rest and sleep his failing strength restore.——
So, Reader, whether 'Squire, or Beauty bright,
I wish thee fair companion for the night ;
And fair adventure, till the morning beams 435
In waking pleasure, or propitious dreams.

END OF THE FOURTH CANTO.

AMAZONIAD;

FIGURE AND FASHION,

CANTO V.

ARGUMENT.

SOLEMN invocation of Chance—Her supreme power—Interlude of the Lady and the Doctor—The plot thickens—Amazon of three tails, her prowess—She leads her captives to visit the Dargle—The Jew and the Justice, two other remarkable characters are intro- duced—Revenge and Gormandize are gratified at once—Feats of horsemanship—Final catastrophe ap- proaches—The pine apple—Eager longings of the la- dies—Both Philothemis *and* Dennira *resolve to pos- sess this apple of* Discord—Dennira, *first lays hands on it—Rage of* Philothemis—*She kills* Dennira, *and*

seizes the apple—*The General hastens to avenge the death
of the slain, and catches up* Philothemis, *with an intention of drowning her*—*She is saved by the intervention
of the* Duchess, *who makes an eloquent speech*—*Exultation of* Philothemis *of short duration*—*Panegyric
on prudence*—*discretion of* Papinian—*A new heroine
enters the lists*—*Her person described*—*Her grief for
the fall of* Dennira—*Pathetic soliloquy*—*She cuts off
the head of* Philothemis—*The trunk is conveyed away
by the fairies and reanimated*—*Jove, filled with compassion, sends Night to put an end to the contest.*—*Description of Night*—*Consequences of her appearance*—
Care and frugality of a little but great politician—
The living and dead disperse—*Discord retires*—*The
Canto ends.*

AMAZONIAD;

OR,

FIGURE AND FASHION.

FIFTH CANTO.

ALMIGHTY Chance, the stories of our days,
Records thy wonders, and exalts thy praise.
Supreme disposer of this earthly ball,
At thy command the nations rise and fall.
Thy nod propitious human glory brings,   5
The sage's wisdom, and the pow'r of kings.
Thine influence first the dancing atoms drew,
And beauteous order from confusion grew.
And still, when factions rage, with mutual hate,
Thou bidst them join, and ministries create.   10
Thee chief the heaven-born minister ador'd,
Inspir'd by thee, he sheath'd, or drew the sword.
Inspir'd by wine and thee, in midnight gloom,
The Polar sov'reigns swore at *Frederic's* tomb.
They swore eternal friendship, nothing loth,   15
But left to thee fulfilment of their oath.
Crowns, mitres, laurels, in thy path lie strown,
Fame, pow'r, and wealth—ev'n virtues are thine own.

For thy decree assigns the class and name ;
Gives rebel infamy, or patriot fame ;   20
And, in a moment, hostile or benign,
Can halters, exile, or the seals assign.
Almighty Chance, thine empire all revere,
The prelate's lawn *O - - - - - e* and *M - - - - n* wear,
The greatest sceptic must thy sway confess,   25
When place and pow'r a thing like *N—— dress*.
Sure, if my muse the future can survey,
Thou, Chance, shalt lead him on his devious way.
O'er his no-schemes thy wisdom shall preside,
His lavish prompt, or his retrenchment guide.   30
Confusion doubly shall his skill confound,
And *Waterford* and *Cork* his praise resound.

Now to the scene, O tragic muse, repair,
And join with *Y - - - - s* to mourn his ravish'd hair.
Not greater fury rag'd in *Nisus'* soul,   35
His purple lock when graceless *Scylla* stole.*

With mighty din altho' the battle rag'd,
A noise distinct the startled ear engag'd,

* ———— Cui splendidus ostro
Inter honoratos medio de vertice canos,
Crinis inherebat magni fiducia regni.
                              Ovid. Metam. lib. 8. li. 8.

And first was heard a feeble cry of fear,
Pursuit and insult sounded in the rere.　　　　**40**
Slender in form, and pallid to the view,
On legs of length a ghastly spectre flew.
A keeper meet he seem'd for Pharaoh's kine;
Or like the *Prodigal,* when tending swine.
A powerful dame pursued him, as he fled;　　**45**
And cried for vengeance on his caitiff head.
No dame so meet for Amazonian praise,
Appear'd since *Trulla,* theme of *Butler's* lays.
In stature tall, and large of bone, she strode,
Like *Tartar** princess gorg'd with horses' blood, **50**
Or gaunt as *Hogress* † from her cruel treat,
With mangled parts of living men replete.
The phantom turning, oft his syringe plied,
In vain—the dame her puny foe defied.

* Let it not be supposed that the poet here means to allude to Miss F. although that very facetious and satyrical young lady assumed the appropriate dress and character, at a late fancy ball, which (proh pudor) was very thinly attended. The bard has too much reverence even for a broomstick from the Castle stables.

† *Hogress.*—A ferocious being described in the *Arabian* tales, who fed upon young men; and what added to her cruelty, gobbled up their members alive.

E 2

The Doctor * cherish'd, with aspiring mind,   55
A tiny tail, that dangled slim behind.
This late-born off'spring he had fed, for years,
With scented unguents, and the fat of bears.—
His Grace, in agriculture deeply read,
Had all manures employed upon this head.   60
From the nice beauty to the miry sow,
Each class of dung he tried to make it grow.
But vain had been the care of twenty lords,
The barren head a scanty crop affords.
Th' ungrateful soil just fifty hairs suppli'd,   65
With violet powder hoar, with ribband tied.
The dame observ'd—(the wish and pow'r to vex
Are the desire and patent of the sex.)
Poor stupid ignorants, untaught to bear
The mimick'd brogue, and ill-dissembled sneer,   70
Far from her haunts th' affrighted Irish roam,†
And leave her ridicule, to prey at home.

------

* This passage is supposed to allude to an incident which
took place in a certain great house, not a mile from the
course of the Poddle, where the rape of the lock was tra-
vestied.

† The officers of the Green Horse would not go to the
Fancy Ball.

Around the castle should her frolics fly;
Heav'n guard the viceroy from her wit say I!
An oath tremendous, by her beard, she swore,   75
This flimsy tail should wound her eyes no more.—
Now, with a demon's speed, and sheers in hand,
She chas'd the doctor thro' the martial band.
Not fatal *Clotho* makes a longer stretch,
To snip the thread of some expiring wretch.   80
And now she reach'd him with triumphant cries,
She seiz'd—she cropt—she bore away the prize.
Oh how his bowels yearn'd with grief and spite!
Not greater qualms could scammony excite.
He left the trophy to the victor lass,   85
And gave his griefs to the relenting grass.
Enrich'd with golden streams the grass appears,
And mourns his loss in aromatic tears.
The lady joins the merry-making rout,
And seeks new objects for the gibe and flout.   90

But leave we her, and hasten to the fray,
The warriors wonder at their bard's delay.

E 3

I join the fight, *Apollo Belvedere*,
With inspiration, waits to crown me there,
Personified he stands, by nature's plan,   95
Display'd to give the picture of a man.*
Fierce as when *Python* felt his arrows fly,
For him the ladies may be damn'd† and die.
Might critics of the bard as highly deem,
As he stands rated, in his own esteem,   100
Few, few indeed, of old or modern time,
Could boast more signal honours to their rhyme.
Oh, were to him such self-applause decreed,
None other flatt'ry would the poet need,
A sneering town complacent he might view,   105
And read with smiles an *Edinburgh Review*.‡

* The author does not mean to insinuate, by the term of
Picture, that the ingenious Gentleman who has deservedly
obtained the appellation of the *Belvedere Apollo*, is a mere
picture—a thing only to be looked at. He may resemble his
namesake at all points—and *Apollo* was not only a *male beauty*,
but a *conjurer*.

† Some superficial critics will be apt to exclaim " here is
a Hysteron proteron—can these ladies be damned before they
are dead ?" Yes, my good sir, that is the very thing. They
are to be tantalized, and suffer the torments of the damned,
and at last to pine away, and die of hopeless love.

‡ Nigræ succus loliliginis !

Oh! now what fury fill'd the hostile crowd!
How dismal were the groans! the shrieks how loud!
Not rival cocks are fill'd with greater rage,
Not quails with quails in deadlier fight engage. 110
Not brinded heroes thus in gutters fight;
While the shrill love-songs of their dames incite.*

Behold! a well-fed Amazon appears:
The standard of defiance high she rears.
A blaze of diamonds lighten'd on her breast, 115
The sparkling plunder of the weeping east.
The racy vintage in her colour flow'd,
A plenitude of form her keeping shew'd,
And with the hue her tinted cheek supply'd,
A wreath of rubies in her turban vied. 120
Her large capacities to combat call,
The gen'ral camp, the pioneers, and all.
She gaz'd around; nor was the challenge vain,
A knight sprang forward from th' embattled train.
A regal mantle o'er his shoulders spread, 125
His form robustious, perriwigg'd his head.

* See the inimitable philosophic poem, the *Temple of Nature*, by *Doctor Darwin*.

Whether the buskin or the sock he wears,
Or whines, or passions into tatters tears.
No part so highly soars, so low can fall,
But bustling vanity would shine in all.   130
He roars, the *Bully Bottom** of the stage ;
Doleful in mirth, and ludicrous in rage ;
Butcher of pathos, murderer of wit,
But sure the fustian and the flat to hit,
Nor yet to histrionic arts confin'd,   135
An author's name allures his lofty mind.
In *Phœbus'* and *Minerva's* wrath he writes.—
Gods !—He alone should act what he indites.—
Yet, if the muses leave the bard forlorn !
Theatric dames console him for their scorn.   140

* *Bully Bottom*. Nay, reader, I mean not any Judge or *Chairman*—*Bully Bottom* was manager or deputy manager of a company of *Athenian* clowns, and, as you may read in *Shakspeare*, ambitiously aimed at shining in every character, and would, if he could, have engrossed them all to himself. He would have played *Pyramus* and *Thisbe* both, and even *Lion*, *Wall*, and *Moonshine*. I saw our *Bully Bottom*, play part of one character naturally. It was in the part of Moneses, where the poor Christian is to be strangled. The part of the mutes was assigned to two soldiers, and it being their first appearance, they fell to work with the bowstring in good earnest.

Grace, beauty, birth, accomplishments, in vain,
Attempt to bind *Lothario* in their chain.
Wide o'er the green-room are his triumphs spread,
And ev'ry spouter feels a sprouting head.
Infuriate 'gainst this Amazon he flew;   145
Three chopping bantlings in his face she threw.
Unwonted weapons on the tragic stage,
Where bowl and dagger speak a heroine's rage.
The chieftain, by the strange assault o'erpower'd,
Bold as he was, to female prowess cow'rd,   150
While images of past his sense confound,
He sinks, a corse theatric, on the ground.

    The piteous sight Chief Justice *Joker* saw,
There where he sate with sages of the Law.
In wine and converse as the moments flow'd,   155
Two diff'rent sides his docile visage show'd;
Here, pond'ring mouth, and brow with thought
       o'erhung;
There wink'd an eye, and loll'd a waggish tongue;
Rejoic'd he saw the plumed chief o'ertbrown,
And hop'd to make the conqu'ring dame his own.
Insatiate, restless, in pursuit of fame,   161
To shine the foremost ever was his aim.

Well-founded aim, if in the public scale,
O'er worth and virtue, talents may prevail.
Well-founded aim, the sail when party spreads, 165
And Vanity or Chance the current leads ;
While speculation takes the helm to guide,
Where shifting islands float on ev'ry tide.—
He boasts the first an argument to hit,
Politeness, music, elegance and wit.   170
But chief he boasts, with soft prevailing air,
A second *Sedley*, to seduce the fair.
He started—cast his wig and gown aside,
And stood a *Beau Garcon*, in fashion's pride.
He tun'd his fiddle, and he plied the bow   175
 As if by music to subdue the foe.
" *Bel idol mio*," cap'ring on he sung,
Fugue in his feet, *Adagio* from his tongue ;
But peals of laughter from the hardy fair,
Compos'd his features to a graver air.   180
I, nor *Antæus* nor *Alcides* name,
No giant he, nor arm'd with club the dame.
But confident, and strenuous in her charms,
She clasp'd th' assailant, in no feeble arms.
Now closely prest—now dandled him on high. 185
Then cast him down with an insulting cry.

Moaning he lay, and bit the dusty road,
The haughty fair, the prostrate chief bestrode.
In attitude of *Trulla*, warlike lass,
When fierce she straddled o'er *Sir Hudibras.* 190
Another conquest, potent fair! remains,
Another captive must endure thy chains.
From the swart east propitious fortune brings,
The scourge and spoiler of barbaric kings.
Where *British* rapine bleeding millions wrung, 195
Prompt was his hand, and ready was his tongue.
But Fortune now, for oft she loves a joke,
Bids him the fair, in her career provoke,
Far diff'rent prowess, (let the major tell)—
Can Eastern chiefs, and tragic heroines quell, 200
Such net, as ancient gladiators spread,
With dextrous aim, round the *Myrmillo's* head,
But finer far, the dame around him cast,
The viewless meshes held the nabob fast.
Thus, *Southy* sings * or says, a white witch won, 205
With subtle snares *Hodeirah's* fatal son.

* *Sings or says.* It is hard to determine which, for *Thalaba* the *Destroyer* is written in a new manner, in a sort of periods or stanzas of measured prose, or irregular blank verse.

But how this net the lady chose to wear,
From ancient records is not wholly clear.
Some authors think, she wore it at her side,
Like hawking bag, beneath her baldric tied.   210
Some, o'er her beauties, that a veil it flow'd,
And finest lace to vulgar optics show'd.
But generous fair, if any veil was thine,
It hid the blushes,—not of shame, but wine.

  Awhile the heroine in suspense remain'd.— 215
How guard the conquest, by her prowess gain'd ?
But female wits are never at a stand ;
Expedients still are ready at their hand.
The silken garters from her legs untied,
Commodious fetters for the slaves supplied,   220
And, what must sure her victory endear,
Her captives all rejoic'd her bonds to wear.
Alike the bar, the army and the stage,
Possess her beauties and her heart engage.
The triple husband, or the triple friend,   225
To please her all, to win her none contend.
Thus harmoniz'd in sentimental ease,
They talk'd philosophy, and practis'd glees.
No vain regard of common fame controuls
This noble union of superior souls.   230

Oh ! 'tis a story that might well engage,*
The moral painting of the *German* stage !
She march'd them off, in sociable parade,
Where mountains swell, and waves the Dargle's
     shade ;
Where virtuous *Hardy* mourns in his retreat,   235
The blasted friendships of the little great.
If worth and honour might thine aim secure,
In manners gentle, as in morals pure.
If plighted promises might party bind,
Or past deserts engage a statesman's mind,   240
Did not preferment still at outrage aim,
Of decent feelings, and of common fame.
Thy just pretensions should not ask in vain,
What *T——r, T——y,* and *M——y* obtain.†

～～～～～～

＊ Such a partie quarree ! The lady—the sage of the law
—the dramatic hero—the caro sposo—all loved and loving.
Amandas he—*Amanda* she ! O rare instance of the liberal
philosophy, and enlarged notions of our modern times ! but
there is something odd here. I cannot, for my life, guess
why this philosophical party should visit the neighbourhood
of the Dargle.

† Mr. Hardy had adhered to the present ministry, while
it was an opposition, and devoted his time, and his respectable talents, to their service, in the most honourable manner ;

A stately Jew, of new commission proud,   245
To greet *Papinian*, bustled through the croud.
Active he vaulted,—wonders ne'er shall cease,
From lottery-office to preserve the peace.
Taught by experience to discover flaws,
They best enforce, who have infring'd the laws. 250
Why thus advanc'd, historians have not said,
But sure, some prudent aim *Papinian* sway'd.
With halting pace intrepid *D* - - - - came,
(For justice in this land is often lame.)

With greater wrath, not *N*—— is stung,   255
An ancient lady, but a countess young.

and they were bound by positive promises to provide for him
when they should come into power ; but what then ? There
were fifty good reasons against his promotion.   First, his
friends—I will not call them, but his college of professions,
were bound in honour to promote him, so the doing it, they
thought, would excite no surprise, nor extort no gratitude.
Again—He was a gentleman.—Moreover, he was a man incapable of meanness.—Add to this, he was a man of pure
morals and unblemished reputation.   Lastly, the appointment of Mr. Hardy to some distinguished office would not
have excited any outcry, any indignation, or disgraceful
eclat.

When vile plebeians 'gainst her awful nod,
Usurp precedence in the house of God.*
For there sits she in magisterial chair,
Protecting aristocracy in pray'r.   260
Such wrath the leech of magistracy thrill'd,
To find a Jew the chair of justice fill'd.
" Promoted to the bench, from surgeons freed !†
" Shall I consort with *Israelites* indeed.

----

* The reader must understand, that in a certain collegiate
church, not far from *Winetavern-street*, care was taken by our
sapient ancestors, to maintain the aforesaid aristocracy of
prayer; for there is there a seat called the *peeresses'* *seat*, ap-
propriated for the wives and daughters of our truly devout and
virtuous nobility. The lady, so deservedly commemorated
by the poet, who is now herself of the privileged cast, and
was the daughter of an eminent wine-merchant, takes her
station on a throne, assigned exclusively to herself, and keeps
her eyes, like as Grimalkin does on the mouse's hole, on this
sanctum sanctorum of nobility. Woe to the unwary female,
who intrudes there, without a patent of nobility in her pocket.
Shame awaits her. The vergeress is dispatched to dislodge
her, without mercy, or remission.

† How the learned justice was emancipated, or removed
from the college of surgeons, is a story, fittest to be told by
himself, and will be told by him, in the course of his being
produced on the table—not for dissection (he is not dead
yet,) but for examination. Feeling the great importance

" Give him the Gospels ; let him take the oath," 265
(The Jew his hand extended, nothing loath.)
" What brings thee from the land of *Palestine ?*
" Hence, to *Napoleon* * and his synod join.
" Some Jews are on the bench, I must *confesh,*†
" But Jews in principle, not Jews in flesh." 270

This said, with force he drove a silver fork,
And down his throat impell'd a slice of pork.
Sputt'ring and raving fled th' affrighted Jew,
But *F——s* the morsel from his gullet drew.
To ********* the half-chew'd slice was thrown,
He call'd it *perquisite,* ‡ and gulped it down. 276

~~~~~~~

and obligation of an oath, he was willing to apply that test
to his brother justice, whom he suspected of *Judaism.* Foiled
in his hope there, he was willing to resort to another and
more certain criterion—a *bit of fat.*

  * He has convened a grand sanhedrim of the circumcised,
with an intention of making all their *Rabbins* justices of the
peace.

  † The facetious justice here attempted to imitate the
Jewish manner of speaking.

  ‡ The editor confesses himself at a loss as to the person
here meant. He finds no data, on which he may found conjecture. The word *perquisite* is *taken,* in a large sense, the
thing itself is taken in a larger manner, by various classes of

Amid the croud a specious form appear'd,
With modest impudence the head it rear'd,
Most meet the stirrups of a prince to hold,
Or wear a Viceroy's livery seam'd with gold. 280
His goodly outside, with fallacious show,
Confirm'd the saying, * " trust not to a brow."
The pandar he of ev'ry public wrong,
Fraud in his heart, and falshood on his tongue.
Well-sounding phrases had he conn'd by rote ; 285
The name of Virtue stuck not in his throat.
On *jobbing* oft the changes would he ring ;
Foe to the word, but friendly to the thing.

the community. Clerks in office.—Guagers, excisemen and
other gentlemen of the *Custom-house—menial servants*—whoever
********** may be, or to whatsoever description of *active
citizens* he may belong, it is plain that he must be some person of no very nice palate, of greedy appetite, strong sto-
mach, and powerful digestion. The editor would be inclined to suppose him an *Israelite* indeed, were it not that
he manifests no kind of antipathy to the swinish multitude.

  * Fronti nulla fides. This character, by a holiday speech
and a smooth exterior, recommended himself to the parliamentary opposition He afterwards turned and vamped his
coat, and made a figure at court.

So civil, so importunate was he,
He seem'd a serving-man of low degree.   290
He bore an empty pouch, which well he stor'd,
With crumbs and offals, from the public board.
Patriot a moment, and a place-man long,
With supple conscience, and an oily tongue,
Much of finance he talk'd, of order much ;   295
And blam'd the rapine, which he hop'd to touch.
Thus grac'd, thus gifted, thro' the crowd he pli'd,
And bow'd, and begg'd for scraps, on ev'ry side.—
But not unmark'd, an *Elfin* warrior past
Shrill shrieking, as the spirit in the blast,*   300
As pale as *Mammon*, when his head he rears,
From iron chest, where he has slept for years,
Him to confront, with scarcely human glance,
A spider weaving cobwebs of finance,
In darkness gender'd, flimsey as his form,   305
Things, all unfit to bear the warlike storm.
Oh what a face, and shape! and what a mein!†
In him was *Romeo's* 'pothecary seen.
Empiric ne'er, from *Galen* down to Y - - - - *s*,
Surpast this Quack, in charletanic feats.   310

* Observe the harsh alliteration in this line, expressive
of the thing signified.

† O quali> facies, & quali digna tabella!

He came, with nostrums, boluses, and pills,
To cure this vap'rish Island of her ills.
He boasted secrets, and with salves profest
To cure obstructions in a Nation's chest.*
Onward he posted, with reforming rage,　　315
The jills to measure, and the quarts to guage;
While Penury was station'd at his tail,
To weigh the loaves and fishes in her scale.
He chas'd the smooth Collector from the board,
And seiz'd his pouch, with all its treasur'd hoard. 320
" Hence, to the midnight mask, and mazy dance;
" More meet for coteries than for finance!
" Yet, (some retreat thine active service needs,)
" I make thee washwoman of *Invalids.*　　325
" Go,—scrub and bleach; an office thine, by right.
" To white-wash was thy task full many a night.
" When Castle-backs were foul from office mean,
" Thy servile tongue would lick the varlets clean.
" Go,—flounder in the suds, nor dare to budge;
" I would not wish to lose an useful drudge." 330
He shrugg'd obedience,—made a graceful leg;
Able to delve;—nor yet asham'd to beg.—

———

* This pun is borrowed from SWIFT.

An ancient Sybil, rushing thro' the crew,
With fangs of fury at *Dennira* flew,   334
" Recall, (she said,) and mourn th' ill-omen'd hour*
" You drove me fasting from *K-l------m's* bow'r.
" And now; if force to this poor hand is giv'n,
" You fasting from your breakfast shall be driv'n "

A turkey-pout beside the dame was set,
With ham conjoin'd, her appetite to whet :   340
The lady from her grasp the viands tore,
And thro' the lawn the prize in triumph bore.

Then *N---y*, lance to lance and horse to horse,
Encounter'd *As--l* with impetuous force.
Deeds had been wrought, of which the town had
           rung :   345
But *N---y's* nimble wit and flippant tongue,

* The fair *Dennira* was sometimes fond of showing her
arbitrary power. There is a distinction, between an invitation to Cards, and one to Spend the evening : the one is exclusive, the other inclusive of Supper. It so happened, that old
lady *R------b* had received an invitation to *Cards* at
K-l------m, and, not having a carriage of her own, ac-
cepted of a seat from a lady who was invited to *spend the evening*. The night became wet ; Lady *R.* was unable to get
away, until the carriage of her companion arrived : in the
interim, she ventured to place herself at a supper table ; but
was reprimanded by *Dennira.*

Turn'd off the matter, with an easy grace.
" Come, Lady fair, suppose we ride a race."
So said—so done, with all his art and strength;
The lady won the match by half a length.   350

   An apple chief, allures all longing eyes,
Of matchless fragrance, and unrivall'd size.
No fruit like this within the tropic grows;
A verdant tuft upon the summit rose.
A crown imperial, that, without dispute,   355
Seem'd to announce the bearer king of fruit.
Sagacious gourmands cast their longing eyes,
And female bosoms throbb'd to win the prize.
Thy mouth, O C....., o'erflow'd with double
       streams.
Thy lady's eye-balls shot enamour'd beams.   360
Dennira felt reviving thrist of sway,
And swore an oath, she'd bear the palm away.
Rash oath ! tho' half relenting fate inclin'd,
Half lost in " Levant and in ponent wind."*

   Oh ! stop thy bold emprize ; advent'rous fair.   365
Death hovers round thee, of the doom beware.

* See MILTON:
   " *borne* on the Levant and the ponent winds."

The deadly weapon see thy rival hold,
That handle tortoise-shell, the blade of gold !
But who shall guide a woman in the right,
When passion woos the prospect of delight: 370
By wild desire the fev'rish soul is tost,
Nor heeds the future, in the present lost.
Th' embroider'd mantle, and the precious arms.
Betray'd the warlike maid to mortal harms.*
And thus *Dennira*, beautiful and brave,   375
The fatal apple lures thee to thy grave.—
Oh ! mortals, thoughtless in this mundane gloom,
How short a step from breakfast to the tomb !—
Not mother Eve was in more longing mood,
When that old serpent at her elbow stood.   380
She stretch'd her hand—she seiz'd the fragrant
            prize.
The fierce *Philothemis* to vengeance flies.
She screams—she tears—the tufted crown she
            gains,
Dennira's grasp the solid fruit retains.
Her rage no more *Philothemis* supprest.   385
Deep, deep she plung'd the weapon in her breast.

------

* *Camilla.* See Virgil's Æneid, Book II.

The vital streams * burst out in in spouting rills,
And perfect love her ample bosom fills.
Fair *As——* caught the friend she lov'd so well,
From her fair hand the fatal apple fell.   390
" Oh! gen'ral I am slain."—She faintly cries.
Her swimming eyes are seal'd—she sinks—she dies.
Farewell, *Dennira*, beautiful in death !
Might powers of minstrelsy recal thy breath.
To win thy charms th' enamour'd bard would go
To seek old *Corney* in the shades below.   396
But ah ! the pow'rs of lofty song are fled.
It charms no more the living, or the dead.

    The victor spy'd the treasure, † as it lay,
Exulting seis'd, and hasten'd from the fray.   400
Not long the treasure her dominion own'd.—
Th' indignant gen'ral caught her from the ground.—
Say, has thou seen a rustic tall and big,
Beneath his arm convey a squalling pig.

      ————

  * From the expressions—*vital stream—perfect love*, let not the malicious reader suppose, that the wounded *Dennira* bled *aqua vitæ* or *parfait amour*. No, no—the meaning is, that her heart was formed for love, that it flowed through her veins with the vital blood.

  † The apple.

She kick'd, she scream'd, beneath his nervous a—
Nor vain the terrors of approaching harm.   406
Was it thy fortune, strolling through the park,
A wat'ry spread, where cygnets sail, to mark ?—
Hither he bore her, with a vengeful aim,
Deep, deep to plunge—but Heav'n preserv'd the
         dame.—   410
" Oh ! consort dear, I cannot bid thee live !
" Yet to thy shade a sacrifice I give."
See *Pallas* in the duchess' * form appear,
To stop the gen'ral in his fierce career.—

" Oh loon ungentil, haud thy ruthless hond, 415
" Nor thrae the tiny woman in the pond—
" Sma' creedit manfu' sogers maun obtain,
" Whane winsome feminine, and bairns lig slain,

———————

* As *Spenser* contrives to introduce *Gloriana* occasionally,
and shews her. as the principal figure in his poem, though
she does not constantly appear ; so has our author, with great
propriety, contrived to make the beautiful duchess occupy
the place of honour in his poem, by setting her in the most
favourable point of view, and making her appear, as the be-
nevolent patroness of peace and good humour.

" Nay, dinna droup the heed, or claw the poll,
" Anither dearie sall your scaith console,   420
" For marrow tint, nae langer ban or pine,
" The bygone handfu' droun in stoups o' wine."

He heard abash'd ; and cast her to the ground :
She sought her legions, with a nimble bound.
A shout of triumph echoed from her host,   425
But much their joy was damp'd—the fruit was lost.
Old *L——s* observed, and as a friend to peace,
Desir'd to make the cause of contest cease.
But whither she convey'd, or how conceal'd,
Not fully to the muse has *Jove* reveal'd.   430
But most believe, that o'er the seas it fled,
To grace a royal board, at *Frogmore* spread.
Oh ! fair discretion, tried in scenes of strife,
Thou guardian pilot in the storms of life !
Honours and wealth await whom thou hast taught,
For self alone to feel and hide his thought.   436
Mid warring factions he his course may guide,
With none committed, yet, with all allied.
His flight from battle far *Papinian* steer'd,—
From care of self his conduct never veer'd.   440
To him unclouded as a polar star,
It bade him shun th' uncertain chance of war.

G

Not so the dame—she rag'd around the field,
And knights and heroines to her prowess yield.
F - - - - - - - - *d* and *M*——*n* by her fury fell,   **445**
The vet'ran *B*—— sought the shades of hell.*
A chief, in cockpits skill'd his nest to fledge.
With bet sagacious, and ingenious hedge.
His mem'ry long shall weeping *Ulster* keep,
If pain and sorrow give impressions deep.   **450**
Where peace of dwellings sunk in midnight fires,
To light the graves of bleeding sons and sires.

But ah! the moments freighted came with woe,
For to the lists advanc'd a novel foe.
With mein alluring, and a *Cyprian* air,   **455**
And ugliness, that told she once was fair,
A faded dame approach'd in martial pride,
And fierce *Philothemis* to death defied.
Sorro wing she came—remindful of the days,
When *F* - - *e* was viceroy, and when vice was praise.

~~~~~~~

* Quere. What Hell? Whether metaphorical or literal?
There is actually in *Dublin* a place of nightly resort, called
Hell, with which the person here alluded to may not be un-
acquainted.

No dame like this to day transform'd the night, 461
In grateful change of play, and love's delight.
Decorum vanish'd—modesty was fled,
Despairing Hymen hung his beauteous head.
Triumphant folly gave an honour'd name, 465
And *Fashion* term'd what vulgar crouds call'd *shame.*
Her house the temple of dame *Venus* seem'd,
The torch of *Anteros* for ever gleam'd.
Abroad so atrabilious and severe,
The magistrate appear'd a pander there. 470
Such midnight scenes the conscious dames unfold,
As *Romans* acted, and *Arpinum* * told,
He seem'd purveyor to his lib'ral spouse,
And call'd the croud to revel and carouse.—
She view'd, but undelighted view'd the feast, 475
And grief and envy rankled in her breast,
The furies took possession of her soul,
And thought presents the dagger and the bowl.

———————

* The birth place of the *satyrical slave*, *Juvenal*, as *Shake-speare* calls him. He describes the vicious excesses of the *Ro-man* ladies, with an honest indignation, but a colouring much too warm.

G 2

In such a mood, and at this fatal place,
She meets the lady of th' *Hibernian* * mace.   480
" Oh scenes, (she cried) of sport and revelry,
" For ever fled—or fled, at least, from me!
" And art thou thus extinguish'd in thy prime,
" Friend and companion of my happier time?
" Consign'd for ever to the Stygian gloom,   485
" And shall the murderess triumph o'er thy tomb?—
" Poor short-liv'd triumph! she is doom'd to bleed.
" For blood must expiate such a bloody deed.
" That sacrifice will sooth my grief profound,
" The blood of foes is balsam to the wound."   490

   This said—a mighty carving knife she spy'd,
The nearest weapon, that the place supplied.
The curls she seizes, that luxuriant flow;
The taper neck she severs at a blow.—
Then holds aloft the trophy of her force—   495
The weeping fairies bore away the corse.
A bust they gave it, painted white and red,
It drives about the streets without a head.

------

* Reader, I beseech thee, let not this expression excite any
improper or irreverent idea—in one sense, the Amazon might
be so called.

And longer still had rag'd the dismal fight;
But pitying Jove dispatch'd the blessed Night; 500
That universal messenger of peace,
Who bids the matrimonial quarrel cease;
Hoods with extinguisher the flames of war;
And stops the brawling of the noisy bar.

The beetle wheel'd around with drowsy hum. 505
From the near barrack sounds the curfew drum.
From far the bugle's shrilly note was born,
Mail-coaches answer'd with the hoarser horn.
With drowsy pace, patroles were sent abroad,
And footpads took their stations on the road. 510
The careful watchman hasten'd home to sleep,
While am'rous cats their noisy vigils keep.
The rooks and pigeons now to hell repair,
To mother *Midnight* posts the venal fair.
And coiners labour with unclosing eye, 515
Our circulating medium to supply.
The Castle Spectre faded from the glance,
The bonny duchess led the mazy dance.

The dogs of office now the scene explor'd,
And crumbs collected underneath the board, 520

G 3

The thrifty master of financce attends,*

Cheese parings to preserve and candle ends.

And officers of *hanaper* repair†

With baskets to collect the broken fare.

Ty farthing rushlight they perform the deed, 525

Their works nor torch nor ostentation need.

* * * * *

* Observe here, I pray thee, reader, what a fine picture
is given of a good and faithful steward, ever vigilant—
ever saving of the public scraps and crumbs (whatever he may
be of the large joints of meat,. or the purse.) He is always
attentive—always at his post, to detect and punish petty pil-
ferers (whatever may become of the big wholesale robbers.)
He no sooner hears, that the dogs of office were prowling, to
look for crumbs, than out he turns to protect the cheese parings and candle ends. While he was thus laudably employed,
however, it unluckily happened, that the pet cats, the
baboon, the lap dogs, and some other favourite animals
got into the larder, and devoured, without interruption, a
delicate loin of veal, a dozen of capons, a haunch of venison,
and a baron of beef.

† *Hanaper*. The *Hanaper*, Anglice *Hamper*, was a large
basket, which, in the ancient times of laudable simplicity,
sometimes contained the king's papers and records, and sometimes his provisions ; and sometimes conveyed writings to his
courts of justice—sometimes conveyed away the soiled dishes
and plates from the royal table. The custody of this utensil
was often entrusted to one of the king's *fools*.

Dim seen, the camp a dismal scene display'd,
The living and the dead promiscuous laid.
In various attitudes the ground they strew'd,
Some drench'd in wine, and some with blood im-
   bru'd.   530
Some curst the hostile gods, in frantic tones,
Some snor'd responsive to the dying groans.
Some clasp'd in death those objects lov'd in life,
A purse, a pie, a mistress, or a wife.
Some, ev'n in death, prolong'd the dire debate, 535
And gnaw'd, like *Ugolin*, the foeman's pate.
No pain to teeth, for many of the dead
Had hearts, I ween, much harder than their head.
The living from the carnage stole away,
Pledged to renew the fight another day. 540
The drivers roar—conflicting chariots crash,
Along the roads infuriate horsemen dash.

Slowly approach'd the commissariat train,
With waggons for the wounded and the slain.
Now, reader, now a prodigy behold, 545
More wond'rous things *Boiardo* never told *

* Author of a book full of gross improbable lies, called,
if I remember, the *Seven Champions of Christendom.* He is often quoted by Mr. Roscoe.

Nay, do not knit thy brows, or look askew,
The tale from *Mountey* * comes, and must be true.
Hast thou beheld, how from their mortal trance,
The troops of *Bayes* † by signal rise and dance ? 550
So rose the *dead*, at Discord's powerful call,
And danc'd, to close the night—a merry brawl.
Not more grotesque, in attitude or mein,
The forms of death in *Holbein's* tablets seen.‡
By divers routes they posted thro' the gloom,   555
Recruits on furlough absent from the tomb.
Though not in hearses borne, nor wrapt in sheets,
Both dead and rotten they pollute the streets.
Their forms may fill a bench, or hold a place,
But trust them not—they are a *Vampire* race.   560
Of brains—of heart—of sense—of feeling reft,
The human shape remains, and speech is left.
Among the living, tho' they claim to dwell,
Say what they will, their spirits are in hell.

———————

* I suppose the author means here some pra</ing gossiping
old beldam, notorious for veracity.

† See the *Rehearsal.*

‡ The Dance of Death, by *Hans Holbein.*

Her purpose gain'd, to *Paris*, *Discord* flew,
Peace to devise, that warfare shall renew.
The Scotch philosopher * shall own her skill,
And metaphysics all the treaty fill.
Or, haply, hopes of peace may fade away,　　563
Like all the ideal subjects of my lay.
But, now, perforce, the tedious song I close,
The bard is hoarse—his hearers need repose.
Farewell, good reader, when sweet dreams and rest,
Recruit thy spirits, thou shalt hear the rest.　　570
And, trust my promise, the succeeding rhyme,
With wond'rous things shall pay thy loss of time.
For thirst of poetry my soul inflames,
And sages, courteous knights, and beauteous dames
Entreat the muse to raise them o'er the throng,　　575
Borne on the pinions of heroic song.
Nor need I in the wilds of fiction range,
For forms grotesque, and transformations strange.
Not *Circe's* isle assembled such a crew,
As *Erin* offers to th' astonish'd view.　　580

* This noble lord here alluded to, seems to have been in a somewhat aukward situation at Paris. I am glad to find that he will again be at leisure to employ his metaphysics in the praise of prodigality.

In ev'ry square and street, and lane they rise,
Important stalk, or flit before our eyes.
Nor shall their merits want their due reward,
If heav'n with length of days indulge the bard.
But I am summon'd to the festive rites,   585
The duchess calls—the midnight mask invites.

FINIS.

HISTRIONIC

EPISTLES.

⸺⸻✵⸻⸺

The free-born Muse with lib'ral spirit sings.
　　　　　　　　　　CHURCHILL.

　The Stage I choose—a subject fair and free—
'Tis yours—'tis mine—'tis public property.
Actors, as actors, are a lawful game;
The poet's right; and who shall bar his claim?
　　　　　　　　　　Ibid.

　Curst be the verse, how well soe'er it flow,
That tends to make one *worthy man* my foe,
Gives *Virtue* scandal, *Innocence* a fear,
Or from the soft-ey'd VIRGIN steals a tear!
　　　　　POPE's EPISTLE TO ARBUTHNOT.

⸺⸻✵⸻⸺

Dublin.

JOHN BARLOW, BOLTON-STREET.

1807.

ENTERED AT STATIONERS' HALL.

PREFACE.

——◦••◎••◦——

To usher any piece, however trivial, before the public, a preface is considered as a matter of absolute necessity; and I, unwilling to deviate from the custom, shall present the reader with a few observations on the subject of the Epistle, which opportunely were addressed to me by a gentleman considered as a connoisseur in dramatic *business*. They are much more appropos than any thing, that my own understanding or experience could have furnished for the occasion.

The poem is the production of an elderly person, who writes for his amusement; and he thought proper to address it to me, as he chose the epistolary style in preference to any other. The notes only are mine. So much is perhaps necessary for the information of the reader. I shall now proceed to the letter, which will be found a material criticism on theatricals.

Dublin, 31*st December,* 1806.

My dear Sir,

After the conversation which we lately had upon the subject of dramatic improvement, during the last thirty years, my brain remained so very much in possession

A 2   of

of the matter, that I began involuntarily to reflect upon
the possible degree of refinement, at which it might
arrive under the influence of judicious direction. Once
entered upon it, I pursued the idea with some degree of
liberality, and the result of my contemplation I have
now the happiness of submitting to your understanding; desiring the benefit of your patriotic intimations
for the advancement of a design, which originates entirely in a desire of encouraging that improvement, in
the principal medium of moral instruction beyond the
precincts of domestic or academical institution.

The first light, as I humbly conceive, which strikes
us on a philosophical view of the nature of theatrical
exhibition, is the degree of vigour, which it imparts to
the understanding of a young person, previous to being
ushered into the vortex of society. It may indeed with
justice be called, *a corrective breviary of social experience.*
At once it holds up to our observation the various im-
proprieties, which upon a first appearance at the gaming
table, the bagnio, or the tavern, with their most fasci-
nating exterior to view, might produce, we know not
what magnetic effect, upon a youthful mind and con-
stitution; but after attending at the representation of half
a dozen of our modern comedies, we are taught not to
receive without investigation, and the manners of har-
lots and sharpers becoming thus familiar, no small degree of artifice is requisite to deceive us ; being so far
                                            conscious

conscious of our company, as to think of retreat even
upon the very brink of action.

And here allow me to make a few observations upon
the propositions of them, whose erroneous understand-
ings cherish a ridiculous conception, that there ought to
appear before our young ladies and gentlemen in the
Crow-street quarter, nought but heroic examples of
chastity, honour, integrity, and such out-of-the-way
qualifications; to which, with the utmost submission,
I would offer a few objections, that in my opinion sa-
vour of the irrefragable. If such were the productions
of our authors, would they not create an impossibility
of representation? Would not the contradiction of
manner and dialogue produce such a heterogeneous har-
rico of idea, as must positively tend to establish an ha-
b tual confusion of intellect, as great as if the courts of
law were our precedents of instruction? In a few years
we could not know the difference between a harlot and
a matron, as characterised by aspect and behaviour,
which would admit of correction only by reverting to
the former mode, or making the stage a respectable profession, by choosing for our performers the immaculate
of both sexes. If thus unfortunately confined to the
exertions of less than half the number sufficient to constitute a company, for a dominion so populous and extensive as his Majesty's united kingdom, our rising ge-

neration,

neration, speaking in general, would come to the years
of maturity, without being acquainted with the nature
of theatrical representation. Forty objections of equal
importance could I offer, but the impossibility of its
reduction to practice already strikes you ; I shall, therefore, not enlarge any farther on this point. Now,
with regard to the other : that theatrical instruction is
best communicated by rigid example—how can you entertain so erroneous an idea? on the contrary, upon mature investigation you will, without even a shadow of
reluctance, admit that such instruction is best received
from negative example; a thing you never yet disputed in
a grammatical point of view, and I am sure you will
not be so unkind as to refuse it to me in this. Yes, yes,
it must be allowed by all persons of philosophical understanding.—What a pleasing prospect!!! In pieces
and performers not even an excuse for complaint! All
so artificially natural and well adapted! I at once acknowledge, that any idea of improvement here, is repulsed upon the slightest reflection. How happy we!
who see our youth supplied, even through the most liberal course of modern existence, with such a fund of
negative instruction, conveyed through the best of channels, the channel of example, scarcely fictitious, that,
let them happen to meet with what scenes of moral en-
terprise they may, the hazard-table, the tavern, the
cock-pit, the race-course, or the brothel; if blessed,

not

not with the power of reflection, but of memory only, in none unprovided with the means of scrutinizing their company. In this respect, I own it not within the compass of my ability, to propose, or even foresee, the least progressive refinement : my design of improvement arises from another quarter, and I proceed to conciliate your approbation, by unfolding the result of my cogitations.

In every dramatic piece there is generally one character of each sex pre-eminent; I therefore think our performers who represent the hero or heroine, should never be accompanied by a person whose abilities or appearance is sufficient to cast a shade over any qualification, that elevates our genius to his or her precedence in the plot. This I mention, merely, that you may see I do not omit so material a secret of theatrical effect ; for with regard to the present practice amongst us, it exactly coincides with my idea, as might be expected from Mr. H——n's judgment and experience. Must it not strike you at once ?—How ridiculous to behold a Hamlet or a Romeo, having his jaws overspread with a beard of reverend dimensions, attended by a school-fellow who has the insolence to wear a face as if he were the grandson of either lover. What a cause of lamentation that even the very matter of which I am speaking, should exhibit to my recollection an instance of the in-

sufficiency

sufficiency of the human intellect; which, (as has been observed of the Great Frederick) engaged in the contemplation of some predominant object, leaves another an affair of utter disregard. Mr. Kemble having anatomized the melancholy character of Hamlet, on the performance of it consulted his *unerring and unaffected judgment,* and, in one sense of the expression, *set his face against paint* with an obstinacy of propriety, that totally overlooked a beard, which might have added dignity to Zeno himself, even had he lived as we do, in an age of *shavers*; its ambitious boundaries having encroached darkling upon the tawny vicinage of his eyes and ears. This, I do not assert, should have been remedied by paint—what! a Hamlet in rouge? That, indeed, would have been a sacrilegious violation of *judgment*. No, by no means.—But might we not have seen a Guildinstern and a Rosencrantz supplied, the one by Rowsewell, and the other by Williams in a grey wig? Had this been observed, the comparatively junior aspect of the prince would have so impressed the minds of the spectators, that with the substitute of *fifty* for *thirty*, &c. in the grave scene, all might have passed without raising a jarring idea in the mind of any one who beheld it. Thus do I wish that this most necessary attention to comparative excellence in the performers; would hereafter be a matter of remark with the gentlemen of our theatre—I say hereafter, for I am confident
that

that it will be maintained with the same rigidity of re-
solution, while Mr. H——n continues to entertain us,
which has hitherto characterized his management. With
what elegance and dignity does he appear surrounded
by the majority of stagers! Nay, comparative advantage is not at all factitious, but founded in nature itself:
very few remain to be informed, that a tainted cod
shines with superior effulgence when illuminated by the
proximity of circumambient darkness.—*We judge by
nought but comparison.*

Permit me now, to proceed by noticing, that with
respect to our dramatic pieces, we are much more indebted to the productions of modern genius for the
advancement of a critical spirit of enquiry, than to the
lumber of a Congreve, a Farquhar, a Wicherly, or a
Hoadly; which might have been sufficiently well calculated for the youth of their days, who received the
good by a sort of instinctive intuition, and unaspiring
of understanding, were content with their lot.—But
we, having tasted of the forbidden fruit, facilitate our
acumen by comparing the good with the faulty. To us
the knowledge is revealed, and daily augmented by the
patriotic exertions of our managers and our poets. The
only objection that can be advanced against the practice,
is, that the approach to a total exclusion is apparently
at hand by the constant influx of new productions;
which

which might, if proportionally progressive, defeat
their utility, by leaving us without an object of comparison. How could we derive the hinted advantage
from them, if we were left without the power of occasional recurrence, to

        ——————— some odd old whig,
    Who never chang'd his principle or wig :

in order to enable us, to make a comparative apprecia-
tion of our present productions. That we should de-
pend upon the emanations of our own age, as best suited to the nature of our mental constitutions, I have
ever strenuously maintained, but must likewise assert the
absolute necessity of an interspersion of ancient adherence
to nature, the better to distinguish the increasing superiority of our art; by which we are enabled to make new
plays after (as many an acute genius has hinted) the original store of matter has been exhausted by our forefathers.
In this particular the field for criticism is unboundedly
extensive.—Do you perceive the similarity between the
degrees of excellence and deficiency, in all which con-
cerns our species ? Of yore our ancestors subsisted upon the almost spontaneous produce of nature, having
very little assistance from cultivation, but now, the
most barren soil, by the influence of art and industry,
can be made productive by due *drawing*. Formerly,
our untaught progenitors maintained their cattle at the
                        expense

expense of their corn; we know better, and leaving such provision to be stored for our entertainment in private apartments, maintain ours at our public stalls with the more provident commodities of pounded furze and turnips.

But to be particular, since I know you require proof, (a demand the effect of the custom for which I plead, and, therefore, one inferential argument of my position) if we happen to sit out a play of former growth, not marred in the performance, pray in what temper of mind do we rise at the conclusion? We see no incident introduced but what, a child might perceive, is connected with what went before and what comes after; no expression but communicates intelligence; no person but who is necessarily employed in the action: one word enforcing the signification of another; the words appropriate to the thought, the thought to the character: or, to speak in the language of an old receipt-book for writing plays, &c. long obsolete: " The mat-" ter rises out of the subject, the thoughts are agreea-" ble to the matter, and the expression suitable to the " thoughts :" Your mind is uninclined to question, and, if the subject be humorous, is perhaps encouraged to merriment; than which, there cannot possibly be a propensity, more inconsistent with the vigilance that constitutes the real happiness of the mind. How different the activity which it enjoys, in contemplating
the

the production of a Le———s, a C———n, a R———s,
a H———n, a La———s, or a S———t! In every scene
what an infinitude of *whys,* and *wherefores,* and *upon-
what-accounts,* arises in the imagination, conducing to
improve and confirm the polemic properties inherent
in our constitutions? How many representations have
we seen from the old schools, and, as far as related to
the authors, been afterwards obliged to abscond *with
our fingers in our mouths?* Not such the sensations afforded by our charitable contemporaries!—But, to
maintain principles by demonstration, permit me to
communicate, as an evidence of my doctrine, the observations which the most recent production engen-
dered in my mind, upon attending its performance.

The piece which I am going to make an object of
eulogy, is such a paragon in its kind, that it is not in
my power to choose from the extensive circle, one
more evidently composed for my purpose. It may indeed be said, 'twas written without any parasitical servility to the understanding; the warfare which it essayed, be as undisguised as a challenge of the tenth
century. Here was no consecution of incident, appropriation of character, or elocution of phraseology.—
But, for brevity sake, I must premise, that you look
to Ireland's Mirror of March, 1806, for an account of
the plot; and, if you be not content with my occasional
                                                    and

and circumscribed panegyric, you may there feast your philanthrophy with an additional encomium, as remarkable an instance of one of the cardinal virtues as was ever exercised upon fatuity or famine. After it the plot appears deduced—but, lest you should not have it conveniently by you, I will at once transcribe it, with a few additions that I shall supply as occasion may require.

SKETCH OF THE PLOT.

" Zarinda, a Spanish lady, having been carried off
" from the coast of Andalusia by an Algerine corsair,
" and brought to the Dey's seraglio, an Irish soldier,
" Killarney, who had resided in the house of her lo-
" ver, Pedro, to whose sister Sophia he was betrothed,
" pursues the corsair in the hope of effecting her res-
" cue; being, however, himself taken prisoner, he is
" sold as a slave, and set to work in the seraglio gar-
" dens. Pedro, receiving no intelligence of his friend
" and mistress, quits Andalusia, and with his sister
" journies to Algiers, where they abide under the dis-
" guise of Moors, until Pedro, hearing that Zarinda
" is confined in the seraglio, determines to attempt her
" release. In this situation the drama opens—Pedro
" obtaining admission into the garden meets Killarney,
" when having apprised Zarinda of his arrival by sing-
" ing under the casement, he receives a letter from

b   " Zobeide,

" Zobeide, the Dey's former favourite, who promises
" to effect Zarinda's escape, in the hope of thereby re-
" storing herself to the Dey's affection—Killarney in-
" sists on undertaking the adventure, but is disco-
" vered in the attempt."—Mr. Killarney is a person
whose character is very well drawn for an Irishman,
whom play-wrights now know how to cut out as me-
chanically as a tailor would cut out his coat;—indeed
they are all of the same species. He is a person who,
to be sure, has such a propensity to blunders, that even
upon his ticklish mission he can't, for the soul of him,
forbear to reduce his thoughts, not to mere blunders of
phraseology, but of practice. Having concealed himself beneath the covering of a large table, he issues
with a patriotic *long life to the linen manufacture*; and
after an elaborate encomium on the table-cloth in the
theatrical style of the *sed*, instead of attempting an escape, is seized with the frenzy of musical story-telling,
(to which the two ladies, *Spanish* let us call them, listen
with the most pausing delight) about, how a Mr. *Some-
body*, " stole from the grocer's a paper of chocolate,
" chocolate," in order " to make tea of it, tea of it."
This inveterate inclination, although not mentioned in
the sketch, must certainly have been the cause of his
detection. Let us return : " but is discovered in the at-
" tempt, and at length pardoned by the Dey, who
" again receives Zobeide to his favour. Sophia in the
" meantime, while endeavouring to save her brother
                                                    " from

" from imprisonment on account of a heavy debt, at-
" tracts the attention of his creditor Kerim, &c."
Here, *by-the-bye*, Mr. Editor in his sketch happens to
be more laconic than is convenient to my purpose ; not
considering it worthy the expenditure of his imagination to dilate the particulars and result of her attraction. Her face being so constructed by Nature as to
have the effect of immediate enchantment, she besieges
the ancient salacity of Kerim, her brother's creditor,
whose character is beautifully wound up by a periodi-
cal exclamation. The *fee* will have him infatuated to
such a degree, that in a musical paroxism he exclaims,
he knows not whether he stands upon his head or heels! and,
to do justice to the *judgment* and consequent *feelings* of
the performer, he seemed to be under an impression
of as much anxiety, as if his heels had been elevated
to the degradation of his intellectuals. Next, of the
Grand Bashaw, who, for the meritorius purpose of
making exterior assumption of grandeur ludicrous and
detestable, when united with imbecility of understanding and absence of morality, is introduced with a full
band, and borne in a palanquin, merely for the purpose
of being exposed to those irresistible eyes ; and descends as *humerous* a burlesque of magnificence, as
ever chastened the prejudices of a corrected audience.
The next object of her attack is the Cadi, a portrit
sketched from one ready drawn, being a bastard of

b 2   Chiltingoe,

Chilingoe, (as Killarney is of Kilmallock in the Mountaineers) who travelling westward picked his father's pocket of his propensities, forgetting, however, to make prize of any portion of the eccentricities of his understanding. He is followed by the Mufti, who being of the respectable profession, I shall not expatiate on the lines of discrimination, by which he is made manifest from the others; the constituent qualities of his professional character being of acknowledged celebrity. But, to crown the conquests of this heroine, at the conclusion comes a renegade Quack-Doctor, whose peculiarity consists in the repetition of a physical climax, composed of a Ciceronian panegyric on the salubrious properties of his medicine. These, having fallen a prey to the force of Cupid's assault, are each blessed with an appointment, politically declining ten minutes from that of the preceding swain, in language scrupulously incantatory; in order to effect " an inge-
" nious stratagem, by which she contrives to relieve
" her brother from his debt, and to punish the oppres-
" sion, corruption, and hypocrisy of her *Five Lovers.*"
This stratagem is, in charity to the impatient audience, with the intervention of a single scene brought to a consummation, introducing each lover to the place of his appointment; the intermediate ten minutes, being, by the indulgence of witty dialogue, encreased to twenty. Each inamorato, previous to the arrival of the next, is
enclosed

enclosed in a press, to conceal them from one another, and also for their conveyance before the *Dey in Council!* With this occurrence the whole concludes. The scene is infinitely humorous, yet of the most moral description, and ushers in a request on the part of the *Doctor*, that the *dose* may be repeated for the uninterrupted entertainment of the fascinated audience. In short, it is a piece of the first water for the gratification and improvement of a critical genius in our youth. I hope, *for the honour and instruction of the country, and encouragement of emulation*, we shall not tamely see it experience any jaundiced opposition from the machinations of a H——n, who, we may reasonably suppose, will feel some jealousy at the idea of being out-done in his own way. If we sufficiently foster it by frequency of exhibition, accompanied by that congenial supplement, " *We fly by Night*," it will furnish as excellent an entertainment for my intended purpose, as perhaps the utmost exertion of my memory could reveal to you.

Now, with regard to the music, it comes not within the latitude of my intention; but indeed it was remarkably appropriate to the songs, and received no small degree of applause from those who are *amateurs* in the art I am, however, proud of the idea of being the first who discovered the origin of a sublimity in harmonious composition, which, although perpetually ob-

b 3 served

served in the practice, has not yet been laid down as a postulatum of theory in the profession : a cause which, indeed I must confess, remained heretofore latent to my scrutiny, yet was I, in many instances, edified by the consequence. I shall hereafter gladly arrest the first opportunity, of communicating through a public medium to Mr. C—e for his future guidance, convincing arguments that be should never compose a piece of music, unless with the precaution of becoming delicately maudlin. I am decidedly of opinion, that in such case the genius attains a degree of energetic elevation, preperly calculated for the sublime ; and yet a flexibility, so as by judicious adaption, to be applicable to the airorous, humorous, &c. 'Tis this, that produces that something—that bewildered relaxation which dissolves the soul in Cyprian extacies, or confused precipitancy so nobly indicative of energy of expression. If he doubt my discovery, let him, but for once, attempt his composition with all the assistance that his memory can furnish in a state of unequivocal ebriety ; then shall we see how vapid and inanimate even his most elaborate disarrangement of transposition will prove, unassisted by the inspiring influence of the Hibernian Bacchus.

Add to these a subject which, in as great a proportion as its indulgence is admitted, has a wonderful efficacy

cacy in encouraging the penetration of the genius, and,
therefore, sorry am I that I have, at so advanced a period of joyous expectancy, to express the unfeigned regret which its reserve has occasioned in my soul; considering, as I do, the utility to which it is adapted in
the acceleration of the grand purpose, that at present
occupies every patriotic department of my mind. What
pity! that *Recitation* is such an object of theatrical
monopoly, that at some attractive benefit only, we
have the opportunity of indulging our inclinations,
however ardent, in admiring the beauteous conjunction
of *beholder* and *behold*, of *describer* and *described!* What
ability becomes apparent in the performer who unites
such excellencies! who makes but one task of *description* and *exhibition*, improving upon the entertainment
of the ancients, who clumsily employed two individuals, the one to speak, the other to gesticulate, in
mere dialogue; in recitation a greater number must of
course have been requisite, yet has our modern invention compassed it with less than half the waste of per-
sonage. On this I shall not at present enlarge, but re-
serving, as in every other instance, my mature ideas
for a more elaborate communication, through the medium of the Dialogues, I here content myself with a
hint of the various properties, which shall principally
be the objects of my future speculation. In one respect
only am I supremely happy—in being peculiarly gifted

with

with a superior qualifcation, for employing a Printer
on so interesting a subject. Were it not for my constant attendance at Rehearsal, and singular aptness at
stenography, I would never entertain an idea of the
publication of those *Rehearsal Dialogues*, which I mentioned. With me remains but the labour, and good intention, and faithfulness in transcription; the public
being obliged to me only for the communication of the
whole *legerdemain* of stage profession; as likewise the
foundation of a system of theatrical criticism, that will,
in very few respects indeed, be found inapplicable to
the nocturnal exercitations, &c. of our stagers, both
male and female, and deduced from the best existing
authoti es.

But of all those relative and interesting objects which
at present so imperiously engage my attention, the advancement of none so much animates my expectation,
as that prime consideration in theatricals—*Pantomime.*
Indeed I consider it, notwithstanding that it started into being so long since, as still in a state of helpless in-
fancy. This, however, promises, if we may be allowed to conjecture from analogy, the future length of
its existence and glory. Happy would I be, were it my
task to advance it from leading-strings to a state of ado-
lescence, if not of puberty!—I would it were in my
power to boast, within a reasonable period, of a success

cess in any respect adequate to my visions! The first
step that I shall take in the business before me, will be
to complete a pantomime, of which I already possess
the materials; and, if possible, prevail on my intimate
friend, Mr. J—s, to encourage its appearance. This
matter so much engages my attention, that I will impart to you a few of my hints; and shall make a public
acknowledgment of any particular, in which I may be
indebted to you for the promotion of my purpose.

Considering, as I do with the most heartfelt regret,
the imbecility and barrenness of invention, that, to the
no small vexation of every person in whom *common* sense
happens to be united with *refinement of taste*, is at present so egregiously apparent in the design and execution of those pantomimes, provided for us by the liberality and activity of our managers, I have, for some
time past, with no small degree of mental and personal
exertion, been torturing my limbs and imagination, in
order to estimate the degree of possible improvement of
which this description of entertainment is susceptible;
and I have discovered that Harlequin and the Clown are
the personages who constitute the essence of the delight
that we receive from it. With regard to Harlequin, I
have contrived a mode, enabling him, by such a variety
of transformations as perhaps you will acknowledge ex-
hausts invention itself, to anticipate the utmost excur-
sions

sions of our most refined projectors. He will transform a set of loaded dice into a theatre, and the box
into a cock-pit; a powdered head, a buckskin breeches,
and a pair of occasional Jemmy-turn-downs, into a
gentleman; a light guinea into a rap-farthing, and the
rap-farthing into 5000l. a year; a peer of the realm into
a coachman, and a town-land into a skin of parchment;
an ignis fatuus into a church and steeple; a thread-bare
coat into a sentence of banishment; a bawd's purse into
an emblem of chastity, and the gleanings of a guardian
into a bow to the ground: with a hundred others equally *new* and *original.* So much for the *instructive* part
of the design; but the *delightful* must principally arise
from the exuberance of contortion, and apparently ex-
temporaneous effusions of corporal wit, which shall be
made manifest in my Clown. I have found that an in-
finity consists in the extent of mouth, which I am resolved shall be from ear to ear, a matter that can be
easily accomplished by the assistance of a painter's
brush and a daub of carnation; eight inches being the
only admeasurement of *true wit,* as I have discovered
by a comparative investigation, more laboured than ever
engaged the penetration of a *Lavater* himself. The
common sort of walk, which we have witnessed in those
who pretend to the character, shall, *perhaps,* be exceeded by mine in *refinement* of *delight. All-fours* is
certainly the most comic and entertaining mode of am-
bulation;

bulation; but it shall be accompanied by such a variety of graces, that it must *even fascinate with novelty.* The ground-work of his movement being thus established, it becomes necessary to diversify it by the due introduction of such feats as have hitherto animated this beloved character; in beholding which, *delicacy of taste* unbends the intense deductions of the understanding, that it may return with regenerated vigour to the exertion of reason. To enumerate *all* must be the business of the production itself; in which will be included, a hornpipe on his elbows and chin, with his heels in the air; standing on his head he will empty a brandy-bottle and a basin of flummery, pouring the contents down his throat; whistle *Bob and Joan* with a mouthful of Geneva; and pass through a number of adventures, in blanketing, climbing, tumbling, basting, kicking, pumping, mumbling, and braying, with others as *edifying and entertaining*; which must prove, at the winding up, of *equal* advantage to the public and the manager; what the one shall acquire in cash and popularity, being balanced by the acquisition of *rational and refined diversion* on the part of the other. Conceiving it thus: imagine the prospect of glory which must invigorate my fancy in the prosecution of so arduous a work! and say if

" My well-earned meed, perennial fame,"

can possibly be more than a very moderate equivalent for the application and attendance at rehearsal, which
will

will be requisite to *get it up* with all due advantage.
This darling theme, and the appropriation of my future
time to the publication of the Dialogues, are the chief,
I may say only, consolatory ideas of my *yellow-sere*;
exclusive of the happiness which I cherish in my regard for Mr. J——s and you, my dear friend! and doubt
not when I say, that your concurrence with my design
will be of infinite satisfaction to,

                    Your Friend and Servant,

                    ——— ———

                                        HISTRIONIC

Histrionic Epistles.

—⟶°°⊙°°◯⊂—

EPISTLE I.

" HOW strange! the passion that beguiles our tears,
" The magic sov'reign of our loves and fears,
" Ador'd in studies! on the stage, no more
" Than cool derision or contemptuous roar
" Excites, each eve we sacrifice to play—
" Why there abortive in each scene?" you say.
Yet Time, my friend! has seen the stage restore
Long captive ages from his envious power ;
With ardour rushing thro' each panting vein,
While yet my youth despis'd his distant reign,
Lo! mimic heroes croud th' illumin'd stage,
Of wit and pathos the Augustan age.*

C

A won.

---

* The age of Garrick, Barry, Mossop, Sheridan,
Diggs, Pritchard, Yates, &c.—Woodward, Clive,
King, Yates, Macklin, &c. &c. &c.

A wond'rous talisman the Stage appears,
Thronged by the genius of four thousand years:
'Twas then Thalia in perfection shone,
For shrewd severity confirmed her throne
O'er Vice and Folly; with instructive reign
She taught by negatives the golden mean.
The tragic mirror to the view reveal'd,
Exalted man *became what he beheld:*
Entrancing tears the living scene adorn'd,
And crowds grew godlike, as inspir'd they mourn'd!
The tend'rest sympathy sublim'd the soul,
Th' expanding bosom spoke its soft controul,
Enraptur'd throbb'd, each breast divinely fraught
With Nature's noblest energy of thought!
Why hadst not thou, ere scenic action saw
No trace of Dickon but his whisker'd jaw,
No drowsy Hamlet a lost father mourn'd,
Nor Zanga's vengeance to a grin was turn'd,
Thy happy being in that age divine;
Ere Nature, banish'd and debas'd her shrine,
Fled to her Shakespeare's and her Otway's page,
In studies chain'd, an exile from the stage?

                        Alas!

Alas! how versatile the human mind,
Still pays obedience to each various wind!
No fine effusion of the soul but knows
Its childhood, prime, its dotage and repose.
A northern sun that sheds a moment's light;
A gleam succeeded by an age of night.
The drooping Sisters of the Mask and Bowl,
Tho' once no limit to their vast controul,
Their faithful ministers decay'd or gone,
Saw alien renegades invade their throne;
Expell'd and exil'd, from their temple flew,
And left dominion with a motley crew;
A crew, collected from each abject band,
That roves th' affliction of a sinful land;
That starv'd on mimicry, on puns, and moans,
Till fortune sent it to the wings of J——s;
The pill'ry's refuse of recorded names;
Misses no maids, and mistresses no dames.

C 2   And

And first, their demagogue* of noisy fame
Heaps on the shrinking sight his ploughman frame.
What strange expression, what exotic thought,
Can grace a portrait from such dulness wrought?
Each glare expressive of a swinish mind,
Elate with notions of a taste refin'd.
A mean conception, an assuming crest,
A sluggish soul by rage of wit possess'd,†

                                    (A pert

* Considering H——n's *situation*, he may be said to
be married to the Muses of tragedy and comedy; but
the marriage never having been consummated, a divorce
may take place without injustice to either party. He
stands by each like a disjunctive conjunction; an instance of pathetic and humorous privation, having
nought but a negative connection, yet cutting them off
from all the world. As to his tragedy, enough has been
said about it in the above lines; and his attempts at comedy are all so alike, that one simile will answer for
any character of the kind which he has murdered—'Tis
the waggery of a grand-papa of seventy, who, in an
exacerbation of dotage, assumes the Merry Andrew,
to calm the whimpering petulance of a captious urchin.

† With insipidity he pretends to humour—with stupidity pretends to wit—the refinement of this, contem-
                                              plative

(A pert stupidity,) that e'er of yore
None but Bœotians and Batavians bore.
Blind Fortune militant 'gainst Nature's thought,
E'er prompt to make her best adaptions nought,
A H———n's shoulder from the plough-tail turns,
And fills the vacuum with th' harmonious Burns.
With stalk inanimate and gesture mean
He inchmeal murders thro' the feeling scene.
In those of common-place he rants and swells
As oft in pathos apathy prevails.
See piteous Barnwell in his last distress
Studious in Tyburn etiquette of dress,*

C 3.   What

plative pun and conundrum—of that, mawkish affectation of peculiarity.

* Amongst other efforts of stage artifice, designed
to produce an effect for which the incapacities of the
performers are incompetent, is a *suit of sables* ; which,
in case of some great misfortune, contrasted with a gay
garb in the preceding part of the play, must, forsooth,
be of wonderful efficacy in impressing the imagination
with the sombrous. The splendid Romeo returns to
                                                  the

What heart so hard, when from the rope appears
A sable suit, as to refuse its tears?
But if some noble character he lowers
To the *base* standard of her only powers,
(Altho' they're sunder'd by so vast a space,
That nought but H——n in burlesque we trace,)

                                        Hear

the tomb of his Juliet in this affecting attire.—Poor
Barnwell, too, assimilates his garb to his sentence. I
think it should be a matter of great concernment with
the critics, " why a lengthened countenance is produc-
" tive of such effect when arrayed in the *mockery of woe*;
" yet passes unregarded in muslin and tinsel?" Such
exercitations as these accelerate our knowledge of the
human nature, and, I doubt not, if made a proper object of study, could reduce to scientific accuracy the
hypocrisy of feeling with all its sable concomitants. Under proper guidance we might arrive at the blessed moment when an academy could, at last, send ready-made
tragedians into the world, with as much ease as attends
the production of a carpenter or a cooper. The small
advances that have been already made in this way, it is
the intention of my friend, whose letter is to be seen
in the Preface, to unfold in his *Rehearsal Dialogues*,
hereafter to be published.

Hear how his lov'd obstreperation roars,

Acclaim'd by clamours of pimps, bawds, and w——s.*

Each

* The signal being first given by the candidate for approbation. They are not so well understood, but hereafter I shall be more descriptive on this head. These plaudits chiefly arise from persons judiciously posted on the lobbies or between the wings, commencing with the noisy application of a truncheon or other stage impliment to the floor; they are instantly received, and the clamour spreads among certain *gratuitous* auditors, male and *female*, in the lettices, and at times in other parts of the house. This is, in general, quite sufficient; the galleries instinctively catch the impulse, and reverberate the enchanting uproar; whilst the pit and boxes, (a few excepted, who are in the secret) remain a piece of still life, gaping in suspense at the bowing actor and the applausive gods.

It may be doubted, however, if this resource should be checked with severity, since perhaps no more is expected than ought to be voluntarily given. His desire to please the public, I believe, 'tis not in the power of the most vituperative critic to question; and the only thing that we have to lament, is, that his judgment should never agree with that of the public, as to the

origin

Each *death, cut-acted to the life,* he goes
In emulation between *aughs !* and *ohs !* *

                                        That

origin of pleasure, in a theatrical respect. Indeed the
majority of the house ever beholds, with an astonishing
degree of apathy, his pathetic exhibitions, and the remainder, with evident impatience. That a man should
be so affected by his performance, as to appear natural,
I am not so unreasonable as to expect. Permit me to
ask, have we ever seen a man dying by a dose of poison, or a perferation of the thorax, united with racking
torture of mind ? The bulk of an audience must answer, no ! Then how predicate of the naturalness, of
the manner, of the expiration, of the performer ? This
is a question, that must remain for mature consideration; and, in the meantime, 'tis but liberal (charitable
at least) to allow every actor and actress to make expe-
riments upon love, anger, jealousy, &c. and modes of
immaterial transition without impertinent observation.
—Since 'tis the thing itself we want, let us not betray
such absence of philosophy, when 'tis done, as to quarrel about the manner of doing it.

    * I was once at a representation of Romeo and Ju-
liet, in which he, as usual, performed the character of
the lover. As he approached the conclusion, having
                                        some

That with encreas'd vociferation tend
To the concluding, ending, of the end;
The concave rending with the fun'ral tune,
Rattling aloud, loud thund'ring to the moon!
Varanes only is in silence slain,*
One poor variety contrasts his plan.

Or

some recollection of the impression which his expiring
agonies had frequently produced upon my ears; and also conceiving that the severity of situation, to which
the unfortunate Romeo is reduced, would, in an actor
of *judgment*, be productive of considerable exertion; I
resolved to be numerically *exact*, in estimating, *if his
quantity of expression was equivalent to his supposed mental and personal torture.* From the moment of swal-
lowing the poison to his expiration, the *ohs !* were mul-
tiplied to twenty-seven, the *aughs !* (gutturals) to thir-
ty-three, interspersed with as reasonable a quantity of
ahs ! at first, comparatively mild, next rapid and short,
but rising towards the end with a musical proportion so
Stent'rophonic and protracted, that, for the space of
more than twenty minutes, the whole house was reduced to a torpor of admiration at the powers of his
lungs !!!

* He discovered, much indeed to my surprise, a
propriety of judgment in this instance, which is the
more

Or when despairing he entreats with Pierre,*
Some house is sentenc'd to behold and hear.‡

His

more to be applauded, considering the degree of self-
denial that he exercised in prohibiting the usual exertion
of his powers. Either some friend possessed of common sense, or a lucky opportunity of observing a judicious precedent, taught him, that Varanes expiring
in consequence of a wound in the heart, a display of
long-wrought agony became unnecessary. Had the
poet lived in these days, and considered, as we do, the
abilities of the performer of his hero, instead of a stab
in the heart, a dose of pang-engendering poison would
have given him an opportunity of dying to his heart's
content, in all the inarticulate clamours and pathetic delight of his *as ghs!* and his *ohs!* Indeed after such an
exit he might triumphantly rise, and, without blushing,
interrogate the audience :-

I have *done the deed :*—didst thou not hear *a noise?*

* If Mr. Sheridan should conceive an idea of com-
posing a counterpart to *Tragedy Rehearsed*, under the
title of *Tragedy Burlesqued*, he has no greater task than
to select a tragedy of Shakespeare or Otway, and inter-
larding it with a little dialogue of the critical sort, let

the

His mountain shoulders to his ears he binds,
His head a weathercock in adverse winds,
Each wrist and elbow at right-angle plays,
Still waging battle with detested ease ;
Then storms the feelings with impeded tones,
Lord ! what a torrent disembogues in groans!
Not louder waves in winter tempests roar,
When ocean wars on the repulsive shore.
Th' *Olympian thunders* of Saint Monday's eve
We think faint echoes of his boist'rous grief,*

And

the characters be cast amongst *our* principal tragedians.
H——n's Jaffier, &c. will then be appropriate indeed,
as no alteration of his usual style shall be requisite ; and,
through the medium of the dialogue, observations so
pertinent and appropos may be introduced, that not an
auditor will go home unedified.

* His voice enabling him, without any assistance
from judgment, to proceed from the highest to the low-
est, and vice versa, he indulges it in the utmost latitude. Preparatory to some violent convulsion, even in
the stage-box or first row of the pit, we can hardly
catch

And sit wound up, without a word to say,
Amaz'd to panic at the maudlin bray.
But such, to pen or to rehearse, would mar
The soul of H————k* or the lungs of war.
Fair Nature banish'd by such tricks as these,
A H——n triumphs and enslaves our plays.†

                                        The

catch——not words, but syllables; the next moment,
as if suddenly transported to the neighbourhood of the
Niagara, " the drums of our ears are well nigh burst-
" en." Indeed it may be truly said, of the reciproca-
tion of uproar which prevails between him and the out-
rageous galleries—he bellows to the noise that *shall* bellow again.

    * See a theatrical log-book composed by this gentle-
man, denominated by him, " *A History of the Irish
Stage.*"

    † The following beautiful lines were written upon a
theatrical gentleman of some eminence :

    ———— to *thee* the willing tribute flies,
Warm from a heart unsabl'd with disguise :

                                        I knew

The next some spirit and a janty mien,
Impel, self-plauded, to the simp'ring scene.

D Where

I knew your graceful animated form,
With all the energies of nature warm;
And yet (if in th' unpolish'd verse I send,
The stile remind you of a former friend)
You must remember, how that friend has tried,
By ev'ry means, to check the flowing tide
Of young desire—and begg'd you to renounce
Theatric aims—*and on a living pounce.*
But I have seen you; and confess with shame,
Your stronger reason mark'd the road to fame.
The varied wretchedness of poor Lamotte,
Struggling for bread, can never be forgot:
When open violence and private fraud
Forbade his conscious eyes to look abroad,
Oh! with what anguish did they turn within,
To hail th' UNBOSOM'D AGONIES OF SIN?
The pallid presages of pending shame,
The lip convulsive and the tott'ring frame,
Were so depicted, that my freezing blood
With horror stagnate, in its channels stood!
All, all his feelings were so well express'd,
That virtue, tho' in horrors plumage dress'd,

W₂s

Where comic genius of ethereal flame
Illumes our language, and extends its fame;
Where polish'd Hoadly in his diction lives,
Or Farquhar being to Thalia gives;
Oft T——t's genius peer'd the parent wit :*
As this th' expression, that the utt'rance hit.

                                        Endu'd

  ·-Was still herself; and rising to controul,
    At length beam'd sunshine on his rescu'd soul.
                                        H. B.

  He cannot say, like Alexander, that he is unsung :
and the influence of Clio over the one, was equal to
that of Euterpe and Thalia over the other—with an
exception of *the sonorous* on the part of the songstress.

  * He is certainly possessed of some genius, which,
however, only discovers itself when an involuntary gleam
of Nature rushes through the cloud of imitation that he
has gathered around him. I am sorry to say, this is but
seldom the case; for he seems so eternally intent upon
the *manner* of saying a thing, that the number of times
he shall repeat his emphasis in the course of a sentence,
accompanied with an impressive application of the fore-
finger of his right hand to the front cock of a hat, which
                                        he

Endu'd with spirit that by right should pleʔse,
And pour *the witty*, if maintain'd by ease—
Should Nature qualify to grace the part,
What pity ! if he vilify by art ?*

D 2   Imbu'd

he holds in his left, is often apparently the prime object
of his attention. This always succeeds, like a set speech
upon an introduction to a minister of state, where the
order of the words, and the degree of respect which
shall be evinced in the depression of a bow, are so
much an object of contemplation, as to bewilder the
practice, though, if left to the spontaneous emotions of
Nature, they would have been, at once, easy and forceful.

* This idea of art in acting, is carried to such a
length, that whatever theatrical genius we possess, is
almost entirely subverted by extravagant attempts to
pursue a systematic something, so heterogeneous that it
cannot be realized, even in imagination. Every actor
and actress expects to arrive at perfection, by *a logical
classification of the passions*, and, *by introducing mathematical boundaries to the various springs of human action*
—although what either is, they or the critics know as
well as if they were so much of metaphysics. In what
this

Imbu'd with genius of celestial pow'r,
If the rapt poet in his fancy soar,

And

this originated, exclusive of the coxcomical gravity and
pragmatical gentility of a certain gentleman, I cannot
determine; but the would-be-critics, of every quarter,
have so perpetually bandied it about of late years, that
I would not be surprised to see a treatise upon the subject, as full of plan and method, as Watts's Logic or
Dundas's Tactics.

The style of this theatrical criticism goes hand in
hand in point of communication with the acting, which
is its object. The productions of this sort, which perpetually appear in our public prints, are the offspring
of an affectation of criticism, and a remembrance of
the mere sound of words without any knowledge of
their combined application. I could produce a hundred
instances of this description, but will, to avoid prolix-
ity, refer the reader to the originals. One of these,
however, being upon a principal performer, and indeed
as eminent in its kind as its subject in her profession,
must, by way of illustration, be quoted. It appeared
in a Belfast print, but was afterwards inserted in the
Dublin Evening Post. If it be in the power of the
reader to deduce connected idea from those parts in
Italics, and make an application of them to the person
criticised or to any thing else, I must declare him an
adept

And ev'ry sentence be supremely fraught

With bold effusion of empyreal thought—

D 3

When

adept at developing a *studied concealment of meaning.* 'Tis
as follows:

    " Mrs. Siddons closed her Belfast engagement last
" night in the character of Elvira (Pizarro.) Friday
" last the tragedy of Macbeth was presented to a very
" crouded house. A Belfast critic says:"

    " In the performance of Lady Macbeth energy of
" expression and dignity of action are the high charac-
" teristics of Mrs. Siddons. She and her brother have
" this advantage over all other actors, that they com-
" prehend, from the commencement, the whole de-
" sign of the characters they represent—as well the sub-
" ordinate parts, as the impassioned, preserving eve-
" ry thing in its just place and *keeping.* Garrick may
" have excelled in extraordinary touches of Nature, par-
" ticularly bursts of passion, *and those happy facilities*
" *of expression which universality of talent alone can*
" *give.* She conceives the whole highly and heroically,
" and *though her acting may not be always Nature, it is*
" *something more (!!!) While Garrick, with a sweet*
" *versatility, might fly over the surface of things, re-*
flecting

When mind, expanding like the lightning's flame,
Is caught by language, and diffus'd to Fame;

In

" flecting in the mirror of mimicry the manners as they
" rise; she looks deep into human nature for the pas-
" sions that agitate, that govern, that controul. Her
" genius does not seem so original and inventive, as
" heightened and illuminated by studious contempla-
" tion, and an intercourse with whatever is excellent
" in grandeur and sublimity. *Were she more simple,*
" *she would be less impressive*; had she more variety,
" she would have less of that majestic repose, so truly
" captivating. It has been said, *that her great study*
" *and stimulus are the pages of Milton; and when she*
" *may be supposed to contemplate whatever is excellent in*
" *Poetry and Painting—the divine conceptions of Milton,*
" *or the grand designs of Raphael and the Carracci—it is*
" *not so much to admire, as to enter into the principles by*
" *which they were actuated. It is to be imbued with the*
" *fire of their genius. It is not to emulate but to excel.*
" (MILTON!!!) Her Zara, *therefore,* her Hermione,
" her Isabella, her Lady Macbeth, are studies of the
" highest perfection. Nature, too, has done every
" thing for her exterior : she is formed for the heroic,
" and, though a certain predominancy of grandeur
" may not have fitted her for the softer emotions of
" love,

In such a scene, his character to save,
Affected courage levels to the Brave.

With.

" love, maternal tenderness and grief are in her person-
" ified. In these particulars she may be thought a
" mannerist; but if she were not so, she would occa-
" sionally descend from that even tenor of dignity she
" always preserves."

" *One of her peculiarities is to dwell on those monosyl-*
" *lables, neglected in common recitation. She is, indeed,*
" *a professor of particles, knowing well that weighty*
" *words require not the aid of emphasis.—(O ! all ye host*
" *of critics ! ! !)* On these occasions she has often *a*
" *striking continuity of sound*; but if her tones did not
" *approach the monotony of recitative,* the *pathos of her*
" *expression* would sometimes be *lowered to the tones of*
" *familiar conversation.* It must be confessed that this
" is often at the *expense of that variety,* necessary to
" *reanimate attention."*

If I mistake not, Swift has somewhere observed,
*that when ideas are exhausted, terms of art must be so
too.* Little conception had the Doctor of the extensive
and improving genius of posterity. From his observation of mankind, appearing in his works, he seemed
to

With more than Nature, where she reigns, bestows,
Yet less of beauty than her vot'ry knows,
(The guide unerring, that at birth she gave,
Dethron'd and fetter'd by each rebel slave,)
'Tween Imitation and a Judgment, she
Lies sunk and seatless in obscurity.
His over-spirit under-acts the part,
Degrades by study and neglects the heart.
Resolv'd his genius shall emblazon'd shine,
With lustre greater than each happy line,
Admeasur'd haste precipitates along,
And sense is distanc'd by the restive tongue.

                                          No

to think that nonsense was aborigines of a very extensive tract of the human intellect : see how contradictory
he was with all his wisdom ! Even now his most positive dogmas receive the lie three, nay, six times a week
in the Dublin and other prints. If terms of art de-
pended upon ideas for a foundation, how many beautiful pieces of eloquence, which entertain and *instruct*
on dramatics, would have been unconscious of the
light, and ever remained in that oblivion,

   Where things destroyed are swept to things unborn.

No pause a climax of a page admits;
By fits he mutters, and he breathes by fits,—
Nor to such utt'rance is his wit confin'd,
His action 's hurried as his words and wind ;
One leg so steadied, that when Atlas bore
Dependant deities, his strength no more,
At loose its peer, of double freedom vain,
Vies in vibration with his wav'ring brain ;
And arms and beaver, as insane, declare
Fierce war 'gainst meaning and the wounded air !*

Ev'n

* I would recommend to Mr. T——t, to place a little more confidence in Nature, and not to encumber his
mind with such remembrance of premeditated manner
for the future. *He mars all with his starting*, his fits,
his reels, that tone which he uses as emphasis, and a
preconceived totality of action and utterance, which altogether strongly verges towards inelegance, and sometimes terrifies with the apprehension of vulgarity. His
ease in genteel Comedy is such, that it often sickens, it
does so *smell of the lamp*. This elaboration of negligence seems more the political assurance of a Chevalier
of Industry, than the self-possession of natural refinement

Ev'n less of Judgment exercis'd we see;—.
The same his Comedy and Tragedy :
To this, by vanity impell'd, he bow'd,*
T' implore the noises of the gaping croud.

Whatever

ment and habitual gentility. It may be remedied by
an abatement of personal vanity, and a thorough study
of the contour of a character, without a confined attention to particulars. However elegance of speech and
demeanour may originate in strict attention, they can
never have a real existence until they become spontaneous.

* Upon this subject I will not, at present, dwell, as
I think the text is sufficiently full. I will, however,
refer the reader to a virtual coincidence of opinion, in
one who has undertaken to be this gentleman's pane-
gyrist. You know whom I mean. Now, that you
have read this piece of Familiar Diligence, need I adduce any argument of my own to confirm your concurrence?—It must, indeed, be a Stoic physiognomy,
which appears alike in all situations : but a face that is
the same in *every* situation, cannot be expressive of *any*
situation. Whatever may be advanced to the contrary,
a defect of communication in the countenance, arises
from

Whatever Nature of *the smart* confers,
She checks the heavenly attribute of tears.
Eager in mimicry of high-flown air,
(A mimic stil l the manufactur'd player)
From Garrick's Nature and attendant fame,
The high-low S——s and *The Dubious* came:
The Mimic mimick'd—now our senses strike
Be-S——sed Garricks—likenesses unlike.
But some, whom Nature imitative made,
Lest that the mimic be the least betray'd,
Invert the model, with ungen'rous spite,
And then mistake reverse of wrong for right.
Transform the errors of a senior name;
Old in new state—another yet the same:
Proud, fearful mimics of perverted wrong;
Thus C——e intruded on th' astounded throng:
And T——t studies, in each word and look,
To shine in the barbarities of C——e;*

Each

from a mental deficiency, and not from any exterior conformation of the features.

* The peculiarities of this gentleman will be reserved until he appears upon the carpet. One of these barba-
risms,

Each turn sententious, the impressive fist
Sweeps from the shoulder to the ribs and chest :—

                     Nor

risms, however, since his recent visitation, is making
such formidable advances amongst our *naturals*, that I
catch the earliest opportunity of advising *my friends and
the public* to stem the torrent. Mr. C——e has, if I
mistake not, pronounced the English initial combina-
tions *tr* and *dr*, and also these sounds with an interven-
ing unaccented vowel, properly, in my hearing; but,
perhaps, I may mistake, and his prevalent corruption
of them into *thr*, *dhr*, &c. is a natural defect. Mimics
ever imitate defects, and a legion of would-be-C——e's
now assault our organs with all the monstrosity of *sthrong*,
docthor, *thraducer*, *sthrive*, *sthrike*, *bether*, *oldher*, *wid-
her*, &c. &c. &c. and even *let her* is become *leth her*,
canst rail, *cansth rail*, and so on to the end of the chap-
ter. By this, *snatching of a grace beyond the reach of art*
we are to understand, that superior genius is incapable
of attention to trivial niceties. If the perpetual reitera-
tion of vulgarisms be superiority of genius, we are
stocked, *over-stocked*, with abilities indeed. The above
gentleman is one of these imitators, and might almost
be placed at the head of the list, did not a Mr. W——s,
on the *thr* score, so exceed him, that he bids fair to improve all the assiduous ferocity of negligence which
                      ornaments

Nor native energy of thought can boast :
In both, the copy of a C——e at most—

                    E   Yet

ornaments a C——e, into the most studious and cultivated advancement of barbarity.

Let us pause awhile for the indulgence of an interesting investigation.

Mr. K——e appears, as we are told by the *Critics*, a
predominant example of *Study* and *Judgment*. I will
not say, that he is the author of any of these profound
pieces ; but that he reads them occasionally, perhaps,
may be allowed.—What's the consequence?—Automa-
tonic gesticulation—a face upon drill for the space of
three or four hours every day—whole pages of tragedy
margin-full of emphasis, cadence, tone, recitativo, &c.
&c. &c. until at last it amounts to nothing less than (says
the *Critic) a logical classification of the passions ! ! !—
mathematical boundaries to the various strings of human
action ! ! !*

Upon the other hand—Mr. C——'s *Nature ! ! !*—and
what is *Nature?*—A systematic violation of acknowledged decency, arising from a thoroughly natural
hatred against the imputation of system—now, a stu-
                                                     dious

Yet no correction shall he feel, if taught
T' improve hereafter by each parent fault.

What

dious bellowsing of half a dozen sentences without period or pause, borne away by the irresistible impulse
of *Nature*—then, the division of a short sentence into
as many exclamations—and such an emphasis—such a
tone—such an every-thing.—This is *Nature!* says the
Critic.

Whether, in these and other instances, the Critics
make the Actors, or the Actors make the Critics, is a
matter that would admit of argument—I will leave it to
the Critics themselves; for if I wished to deliver an
opinion on the subject, I could not, it being anticipated
upwards of one hundred years.—" When a man's
" fancy gets astride on his reason, when imagination is
" at cuffs with the senses, and common understanding
" as well as common sense is kicked out of doors, the
" the first proselyte he makes is himself; and when
" that is once compassed, the difficulty is not so great
" in bringing over others; a strong delusion always
" operating from without, as vigorously as from within.
" For cant and vision are to the ear and to the eye, the
                                        " same

What mirror next with dim reflection beams
Abortive heroines and would-be dames;
That swims inanimate th' indignant stage,
The succedaneum of a listless age?
A *Jack* at characters, commanding none;
A neutral medium between grin and groan.
Not-simp'ring S——s, when amidst the Loves
A ton of Cyprian antidote she moves,*
More out than *Mawkish* in each various part:
Her's any requisite but head and heart.
Her very character a W———n still;
A Lady Macbeth impotent of ill;†

E 2 A Bel-

" same that tickling is to the touch." Swift's Dissertation on Madness.

* Within these few years she actually appeared in Atheneas. What! upon the very verge of sixty? Yes: and the figure and performance were so well adapted, that no objection could be made to the one without an appliance to the other, being equally tumid, and possessed of the affectation of a melting tenderness at war with a *chronic pomposity*.

† Proceeding, probably, from the harmonic soft
ness

A Belvidera of Socratic soul,
No heart to palpitate, no tear to roll;

A calm

ness with which she is peculiarly gifted. This lady is
ever distinguished by a desire to please, and, conscious
that *music hath charms to soothe the savage heart*, in the
exertion of this charm is eminently centered her anxiety to felicitate. Even the frantic Ophelia must manifest this chanting rage, and the melodious emanation of
her distemper is metamorphosed into a simpering song,
operatically addressed to the audience. Poor Mrs.
Creswell! those who have seen her in this character,
will not forget her at every unfortunate repetition of
this tragedy.

She has *judgment* however; and never was judgment
more strongly exhibited, than in her contempt of that
quality, which is to be seen in every hovel of private
life. What need have we to go to a theatre to see Nature?

Art, by Judgment form'd, with Nature vies;

and, had the poet's rhyme answered, he would have
told us that it excels Nature; of which, as every *true
Critic* can inform you, Mr. K——e is an existing instance.

A calm Calista, in her wrongs so tame,
Nor her's resentment nor regard of fame;
No rage we see,* unless the rage appear
To smite some Cully of superior sphere:
Each dowdy stung by the dramatic fly,
As soon as thrust upon the public eye;
Her fever'd brain indulges in a trance,
Of yet a Bolton's or a Derby's chance.—

E 3　　　　　　　　Then

stance. His masterly judgment has *struck out beauties* to which Nature is an entire stranger, and, were she *in possession of a tongue*, she must acknowledge herself every way outdone.

　* Miss W———n's powers are never to be sufficiently admired in Lady Macbeth, Calista, Elvira, and such characters, in which she presents us with what must delight every contemplative mind. In her we see them not as they were, but as they should be; and these representations are probably as perfect pictures of that *divine equanimity*, which is superior to human nature in a state of mortality, as the philosophers themselves could dictate. She, indeed, realizes upon the stage the peaceful scenes of *Elysium*.

Then what the charms that made her welcome here?—
A simp'ring phiz and sesquipedal rear.
Each puppy clamour'd his applause, and squinting
With glass in hand, exclaim'd, *" Egad, enchinting !"*
But power of acting is the gift of Heav'n,
And her's alone to whom a soul is giv'n :
The full conception of a nervous mind,
An ardent heart, and elegance combin'd.

Not only Tragedy disowns her aid;
She's less a fav'rite of the smiling Maid :
With spectre stalk she glides into the rear—
And see! the *Truant* of the Mask appear.
A nameless olio of such various kind
As mocks the senses and defeats the mind ;
The Cream of Tartar with no sweet t' oppose,
Yet sly Cantharides an ample dose,
And store of Hippoo that with queer grimace
Invades like laughter the distorted face.

                                        With

With vast profusion of such sweets as these,
Seasoning *mock-turtle*,* she attempts to please :
By nature mimic, unchastis'd by wit,
Her ev'ry part with affectation smit ;
Her comic character consisting all
In pet, gibe, titter, travesty and bawl.
A mawkish Hardy† without wiles or fears ;
A flat Virginia who erects our ears ;

A voice,

---

* All the jarring and chaotic elements of her own mind are united and bound to their perpetual strife by the prevailing imitation of Mrs. Jordan. We have not a performer upon our stage, comparatively worthy of criticism, whose absurdities and monstrosities can be called original, but one. Hereafter, when he shall be in course, he will be handled entirely upon his own account.

There is, I grant, a specific difference notwithstanding these traits of assimilation ; as small-beer may acquire a *tang* from the vessel that contains it : yet, even making allowance for this variance, it is still but small-beer.

† In order to preserve in this character a degree of the accomplished, she reduces it to dull inanity. In
the

A voice, which echo'd on th' Ausonian shore,

Had prov'd the antidote of Syren pow'r.*

And yet no mimic at sometimes we see,

If act, or dialogue, or dress agree :

Maria's mob, and Estifania's air,

With Behn's chaste diction, are her own t' a hair.

But

the attempt to blend *elegance* with *spirit* her usual *tartar* forsakes her, and leaves nothing but abortive gentility, poorly fermented with the dregs of evaporated acid.

* Her desire to please is occasionally carried to such lengths of condescension, that, strange to tell—*she sings!* and that not only as a matter of necessity, in assuming a character supposed otherwise adapted, but in the benefit advertisements a part of the attraction, actually appeared to be no other than, " Mrs. E——n with a song!—" With a song by Mrs. E——n!" To this she has added *even dancing ! ! !* as will appear by recurring to the advertisements aforesaid. This dancing has, *fortunately* for herself and us, no small similarity to the opera without music ; for she wears her petticoat so *judiciously* long, that the spectators are certainly bound to make all Christian allowances in return for her charity to their eyes.

But say, what temper could thy thoughts inflame,
T' extend the mimic to the weeping Dame?
Sure ne'er by Nature was an E——n made
To charm the spirit of th' Avonian shade,
Who, slumb'ring long in the oblivious tomb,
Awaits some literary day of doom.
For love-lorn Capulet's complaints we hear
Asthmatic ravings :—in each weary ear
How hang the tedious sentences inane,
By starts dismember'd in the feeling scene!
Pert Titup modifies a Juliet's care;
The farceful jarring with the pompous air.*

Or,

* Mrs. E——n's refinement upon tragedy must be
acknowledged. Those spirits, which in her comic attempts are so much the object of admiration, having
naturally made her dislike any thing averse, she hit upon
the character of Juliet as a fit subject for dramatic burlesque. In this design she so happily succeeded, that
it was a matter of doubt with many, (deceived by their
senses) whether Miss Lucretia Titup were not before
the audience. For this stretch of invention she must
be applauded. A pathetic piece is written by one of our
best

Or, turn'd Italian in Peruvian scene,
A Cora struts with *bona-roba* mien.*
O! would some fav'rite of the wayward Maid,
Strong fancy joining to prompt diction's aid,
Produce a character of motley vein,
A half-bred mimic of accomplish'd mein;
With broad dittology surcharge the style—
Bed-chamber incident with *green-room* wile ;—
The just reflection must be thine alone,
The action, diction, and the thought, thy own,

                                        That

best authors, originally designed for an affecting purpose ; but her happy power can render any such, (no
matter which) capable of answering all the purposes
of a Tom Thumb or a Chrononhotonthologos.

---

* I suppose that this arises from the mimicry of Italian singers and figurantes, to which she is so much
inclined; but, like most other mimicry, it is all the
affectation without any of the grace. Whatever Nature
bestowed upon her (which indeed we are left to gather
from its fractional appearance in several characters) is
thus so varied by the extravagant artifice of bad imitation, that to describe it, so as to make the portrait intel-
ligent without the name, was a task indeed.

That to the zenith would exalt thy name,
And make thee victor of redundant game.
—But let fair mercy in our verse be shewn;
Nor give the widow yet a cause to moan:
So lately curs'd with liberty, a year
Or two of active celibacy clear,
We'll then salute her by her next good name,
And weigh new subjects of theatric fame.*

Averse to censure, with delight I turn
To fan the soul, where sparks of genius burn.†

A comic

* I advise Mrs. H. J———n to look to the comic and
tragic parts of this character, and prepare for examination. Perhaps such observation may somewhat allevi-
ate my ominous anticipations—I can find it in my heart
to wish, that every line of me or my friend were panegyric—

Find you the subject, and I'll find the verse,
—but out and alas !—*I chastise in love and not in anger.*

† This panegyric upon J———s is not gratuitous, but
arises from the invariable obedience which we pay to the
commands

A comic starrulet see J—s appear
The secret centre of his little sphere.—
No thoughtful scrutiny of character
Has made of 'J—s a scientific play'r;
But all in all within himself he deems,
And when he beams it is a J—s that beams.
At times in scenes, howe'er averse, he'd flame,
Without attention to his author's aim;
Tho' oft lethargic, when the Muse commands,
He dreads the insult of applausive hands.
His mind too volatile for studious care,
He pleases—only with an only air:
Invarious *mannerist !** of fifty *ones*
He makes a unit, and the unit's J—s.

The

·commands of candour. He is, therefore, under no
compliment for any thing on that account, fair dealing
excepted; as our praise and reproof are alike the result
of a strict adherence to veracity, from which no circumstance shall ever urge us to deviate.

* His manner is invariably the same; the only difference between any one character and another, origi-
nating

The greatest variance that transforms the prig,
Mere modes of breeches, or of boots, or wig;
Aught else depends upon the change of name,
Or style, or incident—the wight the same.

Tho' pleasing thus, yet, how it grieves to tell,
His mouth of sentiment's the Lethean hell—
Unhappy sentiment's severest curse !
(Not *Anti-Swift* could irritate a worse)
Within the Limbo of a J—s's jaws,
To mourn her murder'd liberties and laws.
If, when from genius of extatic soul,
The words of firmness or affection roll,
He make them (vain of tenderness or sense)
Run thro' the gauntlet of his eloquence :

F   Alas !

nating in diversity of dress, and degrees of languor or
precipitation in action and delivery. However, notwithstanding such sameness, his adaption of this manner to the expression of variety of idea and incident, is
judicious and interesting, accomplishing more by the fa-
cility of Nature, than all the laborious efforts of scientific error and stupidity could effect in a century.

Alas! what tribulation undergo
The force, the beauty!—head and ears in woe,
They live a momentary death,* and, lost
In opiate agonies, spew up the ghost.

                                        But

* A sentiment in the mouth of J—s is, perhaps, one
of the most singular entertainments, afforded even by
our tag-rag-and-bobtail selection. Such a frog-like assumption of ox-like magnitude, is calculated, in the
highest degree, for the energy of Chrononhotonthologos; and might probably prove diverting, were it not
evident, that the remainder of the piece is of a contrary
tendency. This caricatura is the more remarkable, as
he appears, on such occasions, to conceive that his powers are of the energetic description; and instead of
slurring with inoffensive ease a turn, which he is incapable of raising to its necessary height, he runs
through it with such a self-conceited discordance of in-
sufficiency, that we involuntarily set our hands upon
our ears. I have often known this grievance to create a
murmur of dissatisfaction throughout many an afflicted
audience, who, I actually believe, would rather have
been condemned to endure the wit and humour of a
H——n in Don Felix or Captain Bloome, than the he-
                                        terogeneous

But yet his comedy has luck to please;
He flights and whimsies with a grace displays:
A native humour and an easy mien
Turn the mimetic to the real scene.
Or in transitions of a medley mind,
He leaves, far-distant, his compeers behind;
To various circumstance adapts his frame
Of pliant thought, altho' his style the same:
The manner 'tending, with spontaneous ease,
That brightens many a character he plays.

Yet there his genius may *o'er-do* its power—
The crouded foliage may entomb the flower.
Too oft extravagance of looks and tones,
Makes grace and meaning sacrifice to J—s;
And rests on grin and pantomimic sport,
And " *Zounds keep moving,*" and on " *That's your sort* ;"

F 2   But

terogeneous gravity of J—s in delivering a sentiment
in any character, or his attempt at passion in Lothario,
which (by the taste of his dictatorial namesake!) I once
beheld and heard him personate, gesticulate, and re-
cite. Of this, if you doubt, I can get a respectable
person to give testimony by affidavit.

But let no satire in our lines be seen;
We lean to mercy innocent of spleen.
Except but sentiment, and let him be
First on your stage, in junior levity—
IF NE'ER, BY AVARICE IMPELL'D, HE DARE
INSULT BY BRAMBLE, OR A PANGLOSS THERE.*

What

* 'Tis very severe that our feelings should, on a
night when we wish to exhibit our approbation, be insulted by the incongruous attraction of avarice. Some
hideous and abortive attempt at an inconsistent union of
the performer and his character, is beginning to be the
resource to produce a full house; and we are compelled
to sit an extraordinary length of time to be disgusted
by an actor, who might entertain us if he would. This
is as offensive as any other cause of complaint, and calls
loudly for reformation. I hope that Mr. J—s, who has
been the most extravagant of all, will, for the future,
stand corrected, and set a proper example to others.
If not removed, 'tis to be expected that the public will
be strongly negative hereafter upon such occasions, and
make that avarice become the scourge of itself, which,
although it might have entertained in Tangent or Gold-
finch, would rather impudently nauseate in Sir Robert
Bramble or Dr. Pangloss.

What ghost, of something we have seen, appears,
Invades our vision, and assaults our ears ?—
The studious mimic of a Kemble's air,*
His tone, his action, nay, his voice is there ;

F 3

But

* Very few tragic performers, at present upon the
stage, are, as I said before, possessed of a manner that
we can call original. The style of the best has been
formed on an imitation of them who are gone ;

And even shadows have their shadows too ;

for the most prevailing similarity in our tragedians,
consists in a mimicry of " *Black Roscius* " This mimicry is not confined to any particular walk of the drama, by those who there assume first-rate characters.
The ancient S—— was not content with her Lady
Macbeth, her Isabella, her Lady Randolph, or her Calista ; but witnessing the admiration which Clive received in Nell in the *Devil to Pay*, she must be a Nell
also, and that at *sixty!* Her Catherine, her Imogen,
her Lady Townly, and a long string of &cs. are of the
same stamp. Her brother's Petruchio, his Mirabel, his
Don Leon, &c. are as strong instances of the same ex-
travasation of the mind. If future performers, and
some of the present day, reflect on this extravagance,

they

But more his apathy—'twould seem he stole
His labour'd imbecility of soul—
The lofty littleness of Kemble's pow'r—
But littleness in miniature—no more.
His native milk prodominates so far,
His best revenge—a folded fist and stare;
Iago's villainy his teeth display'd,
And Lear's insanity not play'd—but pray'd.

(Of

they may, perhaps, avoid marring on one night the
applause which they receive on another.

The attachment of the mimic, whose character is at
present our subject, to every indication of a *judicious
judgment* in *his original*, has possibly caused those instances, in which this quality, as predominant and not
subservient, pretty strongly appears. To adduce one:
in his performance of Sciolto, the idea which he con-
ceived of the character was comedy, and not tragedy;
the weakness of his limbs, in age, was ambling; his fondness, dotage; his intonation, a whimpering recitative:
and supposing a characteristic propriety of dress to con-
sist in an affectation of antiquity, he appeared (amongst
the rest) in a hat that would have graced a Silky in The
Road to Ruin.—*So much for an obstinate and wilful Judgment!*

(Of such extent thy imitation seem'd,
That *sombrous Roscicus* '*self* in Lear thou'rt deem'd :)
Or if pathetic, to assail the heart,
In fits he works the homicide of art :
Ev'n Richard's self, thro' such a medium shewn,
Look'd horrors hideous as his mein and tone.*
Our thriving pupil, of a Kemble's lore,
Renounces Nature to confirm his pow'r;

To

* K——e, our great Richard, in the tent-scene,
swaking from the dream of the spectres, seizes his sword,
and darting to the right, one of the inoffensive wings
becomes a prey to his apprehensive fury; then making
a diagonal stagger to the left, 'tis there repeated, and
so on ad libitum, right and left; till dropping on his
knees over the foot-lights, he turns up his eyes with
such a violence of contortion, that the whites alone are
visible, &c.—until (as indeed we have much reason to
wish) *Richard's himself again.*

F—'s performance is an imitation of this; but, not
being original, he becomes so far deficient, as to approach a little nearer to decency.

To gain the head and urge a peal of praise,
He pours a broadside of accented *as* ;✱

                                        Reduces

✱ That utterance; as taught at present, is artificial
and unlettered, might be proved from many instances ;
they, who affect to dictate its propriety, are therefore
often guilty of great absurdity. Who, of mere common sense, would imagine, that in order to distinguish
words by different degrees of emphasis, they must be
differently pronounced ? Nay, so far is this abuse carried, it even conceives itself able to give life to that,
which is by Nature quiescent. How often do we hear
it preached with a pedantic air of information, that the
article *a* should be pronounced *à*, *with an accent*, avow-
edly arising from a desire of being emphatic. The bar,
the pulpit, and the stage, yield perpetual examples of
this incongruity ; nor can there be a greater instance of
a want of reflection in these imitative persons, who
give currency to unfounded innovation, than that before
us. No one in his senses ever entertained a thought of
marking with emphasis that which is indefinite. The
article *the* may occasionally demand an emphatic pre-
eminence, which is its contradistinction from the other,
but the only mode of making a strong distinction of the
indefinite from the definite article, must be effected by
                                                    the

Reduces movement to a certainty†

And sets each sentence to its tune and key :

Each

the greatest omission of distinction possible. In its
very nature that 'tis a privation of particularity, appears
by opposing it to the definite, without which opposition it would be of no manner of service ; for it is by
the use of it, that one or more from many must be ab-
sorbed in the generality of its reference.

The article *an* before *u* when pronounced initial *y*, as
in *union*, and before *w*, as in *one*, which has the sound
of initial *w*, are also instances of this ignorance. No
one would hesitate to acknowledge an error, in saying,
an yew—an year—an yeoman—an warrant—an well—an
weapon :—yet would many such, with an air of classic
authority, maintain the propriety of *an yoonion (union)*
—*such an won (one)—mountings, fountings,* and *mus-*
lings, is a perversion not much worse. To the ortho-
graphy, when it deviates from the pronunciation, we
should pay no regard ; for a language consists in utterance, and cannot exist without it.

Of this description is also the custom, which has
lately prevailed, of sounding *th aspirated* as *fth.* Those
who

Each motion marshall'd and each action scann'd,
Th' emphatic letter and the doubl'd hand,‡

                             Th'

who do not understand the elements of pronunciation,
as properly analyzed, conceive that this is merely a refinement of the same sound; instead of which it transforms it to an initial combination, recognised by the
English language in one word only, *phthisis.* It is the
introduction of another simple sound without a character to represent it, and by no means native to our language. The contact of the tongue with the upper teeth
in forming the simple sound of *th*, being interrupted
by the previous application of the under-lip, in forming the preceding *f*, we catch no other sound with perfection : thus, *thought* is reduced to *fought*, *enthusiasm*
to *enfusiasm*, &c. If such ignorant innovation encrease
upon us, 'tis difficult to say at what we may arrive
hereafter.

   † The plan which was laid down by Mr. Burgh in
his Speaker, might be very well applied to K——e's
action, and that of his many imitators; and probably
be elevated to a science, by a judicious junction of
mathematics and anatomy. Here, indeed, if he were
living, Shakespeare might see " the action suited to the
" word, and the word to the action," with such *special
obser-vance,*

Th' exact cæsura and returning whine,
In ordinary time march thro' each line :—
Nature from better *Judgment* deviates wide ;
Mere pathos nothing—method is the guide.
'Tis said, some genius of corrective mould,
Who bless'd society in days of old,
Whom Nature fashion'd from exceptive plan,
A perfect contrast to the usual man ;

The

observance, that the same speech, nay, a whole scene,
perhaps even a whole play, has its accompaniments of
position, action, and plank of the stage-flooring, with
as much exactness as a page of music or hieroglyphic.
I know no person so capable of carrying such a task into
execution as Mr. K——e ; and, entirely for his investigation, my friend shall take an opportunity, in one of
his Dialogues, of laying before him a specimen of this
kind with all its fulness and varieties.

‡ In consequence of the frequency of this part of
his action, as likewise of the position of body which
accompanies it, he is (though called F——e by the vulgar) known among the *Gods* by the familiar appellation
of *Mendoza*. This has also arisen from a superstitious
imitation of his great original before mentioned.

The chin at variance with the pompous nose,
Mad moping eyes and *Erebusian* brows,
That with the majesty of darkness round
Circled his soul—supreme in blank profound,
But darkness visible—a frame you'd swear
An Æsop marching to some fun'ral air;
Consulted *Judgment*, and adorn'd his trim
With powder'd peruke and triangled brim.—
Involv'd in buckram in front, flank, and rear,
(A K——e's counterpart in form and air)
His bolder impudence secur'd his fame ;—
While critic genius scann'd his compound frame,
Each elf in pride of admiration cried,
How Art, by Judgment form'd, with Nature vied!!!
Quick epidemic imitation spread;*
An arguing wig-block rose in each block-head :—
Oh! why the monstrous in our dress reject,
And yet encourage so the mind's defect!
But, truth maintaining, reprobate in whole,
K——e's three-peaks and peruke of the soul.

Too oft such wretches our compassion share,
And, pleas'd, we foster with a dotard's care;

But

But why with mimics, of such abject place,
Is taste insulted?—be our task to trace.
Since private property the stage became,*
Has av'rice lorded with controul supreme—
But, oh! what blast of a malignant pow'r,
Blew the dire foe of taste upon our shore?
To whose blank visage Nature hath denied
Each human attribute, but paltriest pride ;
A Caliban, to whom nor easy grace
Nor sprightly folly, gives pretence to please.
Th' endur'd Cook-major of each Circean feast,†
Whose soul is center'd in his scent and taste,

G

And,

* It would be much for the advantage of society, if
our theatres were in the hands of public officers ; of
which a committee might be formed to regulate the entertainments. Any disadvantage that would at first
arise, from opposing the vicious taste established
amongst the *million*, would be amply compensated by
the desire of rational entertainment that might succeed
it.

† The minions who are entertained in occasional
luxury by J—— passion for eating, (the only thing for
which

And, vers'd in culinary art alone,
Hath swinish gluttony proclaim'd her own.
Each pound that tributary wages yield
Is gorg'd in turtle or tokay is swill'd—*

                                        Alike

which Nature seems to have qualified him) from the
most mercenary motives circulate his abilities as a
M———r. This was not forgotten by the author of
the Thespiad, who, when his capacity and conduct as
a director of our entertainments was the question,
praised him for his art of cookery, and of disposing
dishes on a table—and the better art of providing for
one. In all, it seems, he is very successful; his genius
in theatrical ways-and-means, &c. provides for one, and
his native qualifications for the refined situation of a
cook-major for the other.

    We may now perceive that no subject is too mean for
flattery. Even this (by anticipation) " surfeit-slain
" fool, the common dung of the soil," has obtained
his share of it!!!

    * Instead of giving proper salaries, he is content
with those who will take his price, on condition that
such wretched exhibiters shall be thrown, by half-
                                        dozens

Alike a Garrick or a Clown, if made
His gains—a Hamlet or a Perizade.

Since our indifference has seated J—,
Where many a Sister his hard empire owns,
The period comes, that with encourag'd rage,
Spreads *vivid darkness* o'er th' indignant stage;
Obscures each Muse from Nature's parent ray,
In calf immur'd to mourn the banish'd day,
Whilst whining mimicry, in paint and paste,
Struts forth criterion of dramatic taste,
Comes, unresisted, to complete its pow'r,
For we in J—s accelerate the hour.
A H——n's Hamlet, an E——n's Bisarre,
A W———n's Macbeth, and a F—e's King Lear,
The best our company can boast within ·
The clam'rous compass of both Rant and Grin.

G 2   Amongst

dozens at a time, upon the public generosity for a benefit, which was the case last year.

Amongst the poets, our superior gift
We boast in L——ss, A———n, or S——t,*
Our ablest Wits, to whom no wants belong,
But thought and trope, plan, unity, and song;

                                        Who

* 'Tis not in the actors only, that we have to endure
a presumptuous and mechanical imitation of the declining generation :—Mr. T———s S——t having be-
trayed some indication of ability, his son must needs
inherit, not only his name, but his capacity, which he
resolved to prove by committing the latter to public investigation—*but not the former*; the real parent of *the
literary sooterkin* having hit upon the stratagem of *fa-
thering* it upon its *grandfather*, thinking that the public
would admire the piece for the sake of the author, and
not the author for the sake of the piece. Not having
the gift of prophecy, I know not in what manner its
favourable reception will influence the mind of the *junior
Grubean*; but if he unite not prudence with his stupidity, we may hereafter tell him, in the friendly way,
when he happens to wander—See Preface.

Authorship has not, in this Epistle, come under our
cognizance; but hereafter poetical addresses spoken to
audiences, dramatic authors on and off the stage, &c.
shall experience due respect.

Who each Hibernian (a good-humour'd soul)
With studious bulls and flatteries cajole;*

G 3   With

---

* The art which is practised, by almost every comic
playwright of the present day, is to introduce an Irishman as a prominent character in the drama; and indeed
it is the only one that (at least at home) is capable of
ensuring success to *such* comedies, operas, or farces. The
poet in laying the characters of his piece, on providing
the Irishman with his part of the dialogue, turns over
every jest-book which comes within the reach of his
punning rapacity; and by inserting some as they are,
and torturing others to an apparent diversity, a complete Paddy starts up to entertain the delighted audience. Considering the character in this light only,
it would become an object of indignation to Irishmen,
were it not seasoned by such a fulsome affectation of
praise of Ireland and the Irish character, that we, im-
maturely conceiving that he is actuated by a spirit of
patriotism, &c. are inclined to applaud him for his liberality. But if we reflect, that he is urged to such a
subterfuge by a presumptuous poverty of genius, and
that what we suppose to be generosity, is only the side-
long appeal of servility to indulgence, deprecating our
resentment against the other stupid deficiencies of the
piece;

With seeming justice may our cousins call
Ev'n our Metropolis, but blund'rers all,

J—s

piece; that the English and Scotch audiences undergo
no imposition of this description; that the blunders,
practical and verbal, which constitute this hackney character, are, in a national respect, real insults, and the
praises nearly as shameful for us to receive with clamours of applause, as it would be in an individual to
app'aud the flattery that is directed to himself: when
we consider all this, surely we should repel the insult;
and as to the praise, there is but one act necessary to
prove that we deserve it;—to receive it with silence
when it proceeds from one, who otherwise shews himself a man of understanding, and to damn, as an injury of the highest degree, a medley of

"Praise bestow'd in Grub-street rhymes,"

upon which vain or necessitous pretenders to wit de-
pend for a reception from the public, that, if indulged,
supplants pieces of approved value. The representation of an Irish gentleman without the vulgar peculiarities of his country, is never the attempt of these ob-
sequious dunces; it would require ability to draw such
a character with propriety, which Nature never bestowed

J—s rests on such anomalies as these,

To swim in soups, and glut on fricassees.

The meanest stuff that Sadler's Wells affords,

Or ancient H———k's long-drawn page records,

He blends in olio with each feeling soul,

The scene of Shakespeare and Grimaldi's droll.*

Mont-

stowed upon them : but a Captain O'Neil, a Sir Sturdy O'Tremour, or a Killarney, it is in the power of vain stupidity to produce, when aided by traditional anec- dote, a jest book, and the meaness attendant upon mental worthlessness.

* The beastly and disgusting nature of that stuff, which constitutes the entertainment that we call *Comic Pantomime*, should render it an object, to every per- son of understanding and taste, to banish it without mercy from the stage. The origin of its favourable reception is probably its similarity to Punch in the Pup- pet Shew ; but it is a most extravagant addition to its beastiality and nonsense. It has even infected the re- presentation of plays, as was witnessed by those who attended the exhibition of The Critic ; the investiga- tion of which we shall reserve for another opportu- nity.

There

Montgomery here, his fellow Laurent there,
Could more than emulate the name of play'r;
The soul excluded, and the tear no more—
His only pray'r, " May fools increase my store!"
—O God! thou godhead of supreme acclaim,
To all, how sacred thy imperious name!
The only object of our faith, t' adore,
Not Virtue's radiance, but the lustrous ore.
A *Gough*, our bible; sacrament, a fee :
The only tenet in which all agree.

                                              The

There are other matters of a like nature, that should
be checked in their growth. The characters of Fiddler
and Composer have been, of late years, as much united
as those of Comedian and Tragedian; the consequence
of which is, that Mr. Fiddler makes his music subservient to the agility of his fingers, and not his fingers to
the expression of his music. The medium of decision
at present in vogue, is not the effect which it produces
on the ear, but the difficulty of execution. Thus, we
perpetually hear the fiddler make his half hour transitions from jig to jig, in his medley overtures, by a species of—neither harmony nor melody, but a want of
both.

The Mufti's Koran, Parson's Testament—
The earth's attraction, and the flame's ascent;
The same as elasticity to air,
Th' unchang'd equality joint waters share,
The circle's centre, to each point the same,
As near to this, as to th' oppos'd extreme ;
Whose pow'rs, the standard of each character,
Superior worth, by *cents* on *cents*, confer.
The wretched rabble of each social sphere,
A prowling catchpole, or a cockpit peer,
By thee exalted, shail be more than Heav'n
E'er plac'd in poverty, with Virtue giv'n.
From Orkney Isles, to where the British-Brave
Receive loud homage from th' Atlantic wave—
Nay, search all Europe—or extensive more,
Try ev'ry region from the peaceful shore,
And coursing eastward thro' each throng'd domain,
Ne'er stop till peace smooths the same wave again :
Ev'n then assert it, if you dare, that East
Is not rapacious as th' all-griping West—
No ! Man's invarious in this trait—is e'er
The same at heart—self-interest sways him there—

The

The same in China, Egypt, or in Gaul,
At Pekin, Cairo, or Saint Cloud, 'tis all
The same—the savage of a wild or ville,
Gold is his good, and Indigence his ill.

END OF EPISTLE I.

ERRATA.

Page 9, line 5—for *of stagers,* read *of our stagers.*

——— 12, —— 21—for *be,* read *being.*

——— 30, —— 4—for *her,* read *his.*

——— 32, —— 8 of note—for *perferation,* read *perferation.*

——— 33, —— 16—dele *s* in *(gutturals.)*

——— 57, —— 1—for *temper,* read *tempter.*

THE

BATTLES

OF

TALAVERA.

HARDING and WRIGHT, Printers, St. John's-square London.

THE

BATTLES

OF

TALAVERA.

A

POEM.

" . . . . Sibi, cognomen in hoste
" Fecit ; & Hispanam sanguine tinxit humum."

Ov. Fast. 6.

SECOND EDITION.

LONDON:

PRINTED FOR JOHN MURRAY, 32, FLEET-STREET ;
JOHN BALLANTYNE AND CO. EDINBURGH ;
AND GILBERT AND HODGES,
DAME-STREET, DUBLIN.

1809.

THE

BATTLES

OF

TALAVERA.

Dicam insigne, recens, adhuc
Indictum ore alio.

I.

'TWAS dark ; from every mountain head
The sunny smile of heaven had fled,
And evening, over hill and dale
Dropt, with the dew, her shadowy veil ;
In fabled Tajo's darkening tide
     Was quenched the golden ray ;
Silent, the silent stream beside,
Three gallant people's hope and pride,
     Three gallant armies lay.

B

Welcome to them the clouds of night,
That close a fierce and hurried fight ;—
And wearied all, and none elate,
With equal hope and doubt, they wait
      A fiercer bloodier day.
France, every nation's foe, is there,
And Albion's sons her red cross bear,
With Spain's young Liberty to share,
      The fortune of the fray.

II.

Ranged on Alberche's hither sands,
He of the borrowed crown commands
      France's fraternal might ;
While Talavera's wall between
And olive groves and gardens green,
      Spain quarters on the right ;
Thence to where hills o'erlook the plain,
The British bands the left maintain,

Fronting the east, as if to gain
      The earliest glimpse of light.
There while they wait the anxious morn,
Hark ! on the midnight breeze are borne
      Sounds from the vale below.
What sounds ? no gleam of arms they see,
Yet still they hear—what may it be ?
      It is, it is the foe !
Down, down the hill and thro' the shade,
With ball and bayonet and blade,
They charge them home ;—that charge has laid
      Full many a Frenchman low !

III.

Thrice come they on, and thrice their shock
Rebounding breaks, as from the rock
      The wintery billow's thrown ;
And many a gallant feat is done,
And many a laurel lost and won,
      Unwitnessed and unknown ;

Feats that atchieved in face of day,
In Peter's holy aisle, for aye
      Had lived in sculptur'd stone.
Oh for a blaze from heaven to light
The wonders of that gloomy fight
The wreath of honor to bestow,
Of which the sullen envious night
      Bereaves the warrior's brow !
Darkling they fight, and only know
If chance has sped the fatal blow,
Or, by the trodden corse below,
      Or by the dying groan :
Furious they strike without a mark,
Save now and then the sulphurous spark
Illumes some visage grim and dark,
      That with the flash is gone !

IV.

Promiscuous death around they send,
Foe falls by foe, and friend by friend,

Heaped in that narrow plain.
But, with the dawn, the victors view
Ten gallant French the valley strew
    For every Briton slain:
They view with not unmingled pride—
Some anxious thoughts their souls divide,
  Another victory's still to gain,
A fiercer field must yet be tried,
Hundreds of foes they see have died,
    But thousands still remain.
From the hill summit they behold,
Tipped with the morning's orient gold,
    And swarming o'er the field,
Full fifty thousand muskets bright,
Led by old warriors trained to fight
    And all in conquest skilled :
With twice their number doomed to try
The unequal war, brave souls ! they cry,
" Conquer we may, perhaps must die,
    " But never, never yield."

V.

Thus ardent they : but who can tell,
In Wellesley's heart what passions swell,
What cares must agitate his mind,
What wishes, doubts and hopes combined,
Whom with his country's chosen bands,
'Midst cold allies, in foreign lands,

Outnumb'ring foes surround ;
From whom that country's jealous call,
Demands the blood, the fame of all ;
To whom 'twere not enough to fall,

Unless with victory crowned.
Oh heart of honour, soul of fire,
Even at that moment fierce and dire,

Thy agony of fame !
When Britain's fortune dubious hung,
And France tremendous swept along,

In tides of blood and flame :
Even while thy genius and thy arm
Retrieved the day and turned the storm,

Even at that moment, factious spite,
And envious fraud essayed to blight
  The honours of thy name.

VI.

He thinks not of them ;—from that height
He views the scene of future fight,
And, silent and serene, surveys
Down to the plain where Tajo strays,
The woods, the streams, the mountain ways,
  Each dell and sylvan hold :
And all his gallant chiefs around
Observant watch, where o'er the ground
  His eagle glance has rolled.
Few words he spake, or needed they,
Where to condense the loose array,
  Or where the line unfold ;
They saw, they felt, what he would say,
And the best order of that day,
  It was his eye that told.

Prophetic, to each chief he shows,
On wing or center, where the foes
     Will pour their fury most ;
Points out what portion of the field
To their advance 'twere good to yield,
     And what must not be lost.
' Away, away ! the adverse power
     ' Marshals, and moves his host.
' 'Tis come, 'tis come, the trial hour,
     ' Each to his destined post.
' And when you charge, be this your cry,
' Britons strike home, and win or die,—
     ' The grave or victory !'

VII.

And is it now a goodly sight,
     Or dreadful to behold,
The pomp of that approaching fight,
Waving ensigns, pennons light,
And gleaming blades and bayonets bright,

And eagles winged with gold ;
And warrior bands of many a hue,
Scarlet and white and green and blue,
Like rainbows, o'er the morning dew,
　　Their varied lines unfold :
While cymbal clang and trumpet strain,
　　The knell of battle toll'd ;
And trampling squadrons beat the plain,
'Till the clouds echoed back again,
　　As if the thunder rolled.

VIII.

Soon, soon must vanish that array,
Those varied colours fade away,
And eagle bright and pennon gay,
　　With bloody dust be soiled ;
Soon, soon be hushed in various death,
The cymbal's clang, the trumpet's breath,
　　And shouts of warriors wild.

Thousands shall fall of every force,
English and French, and foot and horse,
  In mingled carnage piled.
And distant lands shall share the woe,
Nor Tajo's stream alone shall flow,
  With this day's grief defiled.—
On Severn's banks, and Loire's and Rhine's,
Full many a weeping victim pines,
And longs, the news it dreads, to hear,
  And trembles and desires—
Wives for their husbands, pray and fear,
And parents for their children dear,
  And children for their sires :
Long shall they pine, and fear, and pray—
Many are doomed to death to-day,
Whose fate shall ne'er at home be told ;
Whose very names the grave shall fold,
Many, for whose return in vain
The wistful eye of love shall strain,

In vain, parental fondness sigh,
    And filial sorrow mourn—
On Talavera's plain they lie,
    No ! never to return !

IX.

But, tyrant, thou, whose ruthless wile
  It was to sap Iberia's throne,
With oaths confiding youth beguile,
  Cheat thy sworn ally of his crown,
  Chain him in treacherous dungeon down,
And Bourbon's hallowed seat defile
  With a base puppet of thine own—
Thou yet shalt feel the vengeance due
    To him who swears but to betray,
Who never aids but to undo,
    And only smiles to slay !
In thy last hour of parting pain,
    The parents', widow's, orphan's moan,

The shrieking of the battle plain,
        The murdered prisoners' midnight groan,
Shall harrow up thy brain ;
Millions by thee untimely slain,
        Thou peopler of the tomb,
Shall rise upon thy frensied view—
See, D'Enghien leads the shadowy crew,
And stern and silent 'midst their cries,
Shakes the curst torches in thine eyes
        That lighted to his doom !

X.

Yet, ere that hour, there's vengeance still,
And Talavera's stubborn hill
        Shall cost thee many a pang
Of anxious fear and wounded pride ;
Tho' over half the world beside,
        Thy chains of conquest clang,
Tho' empires at thy footstool cower,

Still Spain and England brave thy power;
In faith and victory knit, they shroud
Thy fame, and with a thunder cloud,
    Thy destiny o'erhang!

XI.

Yes, ere that hour, there's vengeance still—
For now towards Talavera's hill
    The Gallic columns haste;
The same they are, and led by those,
The scourges of the world's repose,
Victors of Milan's fair domain,
Of Austerlitz's wintery plain,
    And Friedland's dreary waste:
Who Prussia's shivered sceptre hurled
Down to the earth, and from the world
    Her very name erased:
Who boast them, in presumptuous tone,
Each feat and fortune to have known

Of war, except defeat alone ;
  But now of that to taste !
For Him, long tried in battle storms,
  Him, who in Ind's unequal war,
Scattered, like dust, the sable swarms
  Of Scindiah and Berar ;
Him, conqueror still where'er he turns,
  Whether on Zealand's frozen reign,
Or where the sultry summer burns
  Vimero's Lusitanian plain ;
Who, from his tyrant station shook
With grasp of steel, Abrantes' Duke ;
Who, from old Douro's rescued side,
Dispersed Dalmatia's upstart pride ;
Him, not Sebastiani's wile,
  Nor practiced Jourdan's veteran fame,
  Nor Victor ! thy portentous name
In this day's fight shall foil.

XII.

Valiant tho' vain, tho' boastful wise,
Marshalls, and Dukes ! with skilful eyes
    You view the allied line.
And well your prudent councils weigh
The eventful danger of that day,
Where Wellesley's star's terrific ray,
    And Britain's red-cross shine.
And while they shine, tho' you should foil
The Spanish spear, 'twere fruitless toil—
    Not half a victory !
Nothing is done, 'till Britain's spoil
    On France's crest you see.
Full then on her the torrent course
Of battle drive, and all your force,
    Your universal train
Expend on her, and her alone,
Be the whole gathered storm her own,

Her peril and her pain !
Press her with growing thousands round,
Dash that red banner to the ground,
    And seal the fate of Spain !

XIII.

Now from the dark artillery broke
Lightning flash and thunder stroke ;
And volumed clouds of fiery smoke
    Roll in the darkened air :
Wrapped in its shade, unheard, unseen,
Artful surprize, and onset keen,
    The nimble French prepare.
On the whole allied line they throw
    Their wide extended host,
Center and left and right, nor show
    What point they threaten most.
But Wellesley undeceived, the brunt
Of war, expects on Britain's front,

But strengthens most the vaward ranks
That hang along the mountain banks,
For well he judges, Gallia still
Is bent to seize that bloodstained hill,
Strain all her force, exhaust her skill,
      To plant her eagles there;
That soon, from that commanding height
May speed their devastating flight,
And, sweeping o'er the scattered plain,
The hopes of England and of Spain
      With iron talon tear.

XIV.

Three columns of the flower of France,
With rapid step and firm, advance,
      At first thro' tangled ground,
O'er fence and dell and deep ravine—
At length they reach the level green,
The midnight battle's murderous scene,

C

The valley's eastern bound.
There in a rapid line they form,
Thence are just rushing to the storm
    By bold Belluno led,
When sudden thunders shake the vale,
Day seems, as in eclipse, to fail,
    The light of heaven is fled ;
A dusty whirlwind rides the sky,
A living tempest rushes by
    With deafening clang and tread—
' A charge, a charge,' the British cry,
    ' And Seymour at its head.'

XV.

Belluno sees the coming storm,
    And feels the instant need.
' Break up the line, the column form,
    ' And break and form with speed,
' Or under Britain's thundering arm
    ' In rout and ruin bleed.'

Quick, as the haste of his commands,

The lengthened lines are gone,

And broken into nimble bands

Across the plain they run ;

' Spur, Britain, spur thy foaming horse,

' O'ertake them in their scattered course

' And sweep them from the land !'

She spurs, she flies ; in vain, in vain—

Already they have passed the plain,

And now the broken ground they gain,

And now, a column, stand !

' Rein up thy courser, Britain, rein !'—

But who the tempest can restrain ?

The mountain flood command ?

Down the ravine, with hideous crash,

Headlong the foremost squadrons dash,

And many a soldier, many a steed

Crushed in the dire confusion bleed.

The rest, as ruin fills the trench,

Pass clear, and on the columned French,

A broken and tumultuous throng
With glorious rashness dash along,
  Too prodigal of life ;
And they had died, aye every one,
But Wellesley cries, ' On, Anson, on,
' Langworth, and Albuquerque and **Payne,**
' Lead Britain, Hanover and Spain,
  ' And turn th' unequal strife.'

XVI.

Now from the plain and every steep
  A thousand thunders peal ;
Again the vollied tempests sweep,
And sulphury vapours dark and deep
  The meeting armies veil ;
The kindling fight at every post
Blazes, but towards the centre most,
Whence, hoping on a happier stage,
The renovated war to wage,
  France now assails the hill,

And pours with aggregated rage
  The storm of fire and steel ;
And when the freshening breezes broke
A chasm in the volumed smoke,
Busy and black was seen to wave
  The iron harvest of the field,—
  That harvest, which in slaughter tilled,
Is gathered in the grave :—
And now before their mutual fires
  They yield, and now advance ;
And now 'tis Britain that retires,
  And now the line of France :
They struggle long with changeful fate,
  And all the battle's various cries
Now depressed, and now elate,
  In mingled clamours rise;
Till France at length before the weight
  Of British onset flies :
‘ Forward,’ the fiery victors shout,
‘ Forward, the enemy's in rout,
  ‘ Pursue him and he dies !’

XVII.

Hot and impetuous they pursued,
And wild with carnage, drunk with blood,
    Rushed on the plain below ;
The wily Frenchman saw and stood—
Screened by the verges of the wood
    He turned him on the foe.
The gallant bands that guard the crown
Of England, led the battle down,
    And in their furious mood
Thrice they essayed with onset fierce,
Thrice failed, collected France to pierce—
    Still France collected, stood.
While full on each uncovered flank
Cannon and mortar swept their rank,
And many a generous Briton sank
    Before the dreadful blaze ;
Yet 'midst that dreadful blaze and din
    Their fearless shout they raise,

And ever, as their numbers thin,
Fresh spirits, to the post, rush in
     Of peril and of praise.
And still as with a blacker shade
     Fortune obscures the day ;
Commingled thro' the fight they wade,
And hand to hand and blade to blade,
Their blind and furious efforts braid,
As if, still dark and disarrayed,
     They fought the midnight fray.

XVIII.

In vain.—New hopes and fresher force
Inspirit France, and urge her course,
A torrent rapid wild and hoarse,
     On Briton's wavering train.
As when, before the wintery skies,
The struggling forests sink and rise,
     And rise and sink again,
While the gale scatters as it flies
     Their ruins o'er the plain ;

Before the tempest of her foes,
So England sank, and England rose,
And, tho' still rooted in the vale,
Strewed her rent branches on the gale.
Then, Wellesley ! on thy tortured thought
  What honest anguish crost !
Oh how thy generous bosom burned,
To see even by a glorious fault
The flowing tide of victory turned,
  And Spain and England lost !—
Lost, but that as the peril great,
And rising on the storms of fate
  His rapid genius soars,
Sees, at a glance, his whole resource,
Drains from each stronger point its force,
  And on the weaker pours :
Present where'er his soldiers bleed,
  He rushes thro' the fray,
And, so the dangerous chances need,
In high emprize and desperate deed,
  Squanders himself away !

XIX.

Now from the summit, at his call,
  A gallant legion, firm and slow
Advances on victorious Gaul ;
Undaunted tho' their comrades fall !
  Unshaken tho' their leader's low !
Fixed—as the high and buttressed mound,
That guards some leaguered city round,
They stand unmoved—behind them form
The flying fragments of the storm ;
While on their sheltering front, amain
France drives, with all her thundering train,
  Her full career of death.
But drives in vain—for unimpressed,
The arm of havoc they arrest,
And from the foe's exulting crest,
  Tear down the laurel wreath ;
Nor does the gallant foe resign
  A tame inglorious prize ;
Long, long on Britain's rallied line
  The deadly fire he plies ;

Long, long where Britain's banners shine,
  He vainly toils and dies !—
Ne'er to a battle's fiercer groan
  Did mountain echoes roar,
Nor ever evening blush upon
  A redder field of gore.
But feebler now, and feebler still
The panting French assail the hill,
And weaker grows their cannon's roar,
And thinner falls their musket shower,
  Fainter their clanging steel ;
They shout, they charge, they stand no more—
And staggering in the slippery gore,
  Their very leaders reel.

XX.

But shooting high and rolling far,
What new and horrid face of war
  Now flushes on the sight ?

'Tis France, as furious she retires,
That wreaks in desolating fires,
    The vengeance of her flight.
The flames the grassy vale o'er-run,
Already parched by summer's sun ;
And sweeping turbid down the breeze
In clouds the arid thickets seize,
And climb the dry and withered trees
    In flashes long and bright.
Oh ! 'twas a scene sublime and dire,
To see that billowy sea of fire,
Rolling its fierce and flakey flood,
O'er cultured field and tangled wood,
And drowning in the flaming tide,
Autumn's hope and summer's pride.
From Talavera's wall and tower
    And from the mountain's height,
Where they had stood for many an hour,
    To view the varying fight,
Burghers and peasants in amaze
Behold their groves and vineyards blaze ;

Trembling they viewed the bloody fray,
But little thought, ere close of day,
That England's sigh and France's groan
Should be re-echoed by their own !
But ah ! far other cries than these
Are wafted on the dismal breeze—
Groans, not the wounded's lingering groan—
Shrieks, not the shriek of death alone—
But groan and shriek and horrid yell
    Of terror, torture, and despair,
Such as 'twould freeze the tongue to tell,
    And chill the heart to hear,
When to the very field of fight,
Dreadful alike in sound and sight,
    The conflagration spread,
Involving in its fiery wave,
The brave and reliques of the brave—
    The dying and the dead !

XXI.

And now again the evening sheds
　　　Her dewy veil on Tajo's side,
And from the Sierra's rocky heads,
　　　The giant shadows stride.
And all is dim and dark again—
Save here and there upon the plain,
　　　As if from funeral pyres,
Casting a dull and flickering light
Across the umbered face of night,
　　　Still flash the baleful fires.
But since the close of yester-e'en
How altered is the martial scene :
Again, in night's surrounding veil,
　　　France moves her busy bands—but now
She comes not, venturous, to assail
The victors in their guarded vale,
　　　Or on the mountain's brow—
No ! baffled and disheartened, o'er
Alberche's stream, and from his shore,

With silent haste she speeds,
Nor dares, e'en at that midnight hour,
    To take the rest she needs ;
Far from the tents where late she lay,
Far from the field where late she fought,
With rapid step and humbled thought,
    All night she holds her way :
Leaving to Britain's conquering sons,
Standards rent and ponderous guns,
    The trophies of the fray !
The weak, the wounded, and the slain—
The triumph of the battle plain—
    The glory of the day !

XXII.

I would not check the tender sigh,
    I would not chide the pious tear,
That heaves the heart and dims the eye,
    When honoured friend and kinsman dear,
    Even upon victory's proudest bier,
Loved, lost, lamented, lie !

But I would say, for those that die
   In honour's high career,
For those in glory's grave who sleep,
Weep fondly, but, exulting, weep!
The fairest wreath that fame can bind,
Is ever with the cypress twined;
And fresher from th' untimely tomb
Renown's eternal laurels bloom;
Fickle is fortune and unsure,
And worth and fame to be secure
   Must be in death enshrined!
I too have known what 'tis to part
With the first inmate of my heart;
To feel the bonds of nature riven,
   To witness o'er the glowing dawn,
The spring of youth, the fire of heaven,
   The grave's deep shadows drawn!
He slept not on the battle plain
   The slumber of the brave—
Worn with disease, and racked with pain,
   Far o'er th' Atlantic wave

He sought eluding health – in vain—
Health never lit his eye again,
   He fills a foreign grave !
Oh, had he lived, his hand to-day
   Had woven for the victor's brow,
Such chaplet as the enthusiast lay
   Of genius may bestow ;
Or, since 'twas Heaven's severer doom
To call him to an early tomb ;
Would, Wellesley, would that he had died
Beneath thine eye and at thy side !
It would have lightened sorrow's load,
Had thy applause on him bestowed
   The fame he loved in thee ;
And reared his honoured tomb beside
Those of the gallant hearts who died,
Their kinsmen's, friends', and country's pride,
   In Talavera's victory.

NOTES.

STANZA II. l. 2. *He of the barrowed crown.*
"The *borrowed* Majesty of Denmark."

Hamlet.

Joseph (el Rey botilla) was in the field, and of course nominally commanding in chief ; but he seems very prudently to have placed himself opposite to the Spanish lines, where there was little to do, and, accordingly, we do not hear of him again, till his gasconading proclamations from Saint Olalla, *after his retreat.*

St. III. l. 1. *Thrice they come on.* I have taken the liberty of representing the three attacks on General Hill's position to have been all made about midnight, and in immediate succession, though, in fact, the first occurred late in the evening, the second only at midnight, and the third about day break on the 28th.

St. III. l. 8. *Peter's Holy Aisle.* The abbey church of Westminster, dedicated to St. Peter.

St. IV. l. 1. *Promiscuous Death.* It is certain that in the confusion of the night fight, much loss was occasioned on both parts, by mistaking friends for foes.

D

St. IV. l. 16. *Fifty thousand muskets.* The French acknowledge to have had 45,000 men engaged, and we know that the effective British scarcely, if at all, exceeded 20,000.

St. V. l. 14. *Thy agony of fame.* This expression, and another in the last line of the XVIIIth Stanza, are borrowed from a splendid passage of Mr. Burke's, in which, speaking of Lord Keppel, he says, " With what zeal and anxious affection I attended him through his trial, *that agony of his glory,*— with what prodigality I *squandered* myself in courting almost every sort of enmity for his sake ;" &c. *Burke's Works,* v. 8. p. 64.

St. V. l. 20. *Factious spite.* The calumniators of Sir Arthur Wellesley have been so industrious in publishing their malignity, that it is unnecessary to recall to the public observation any particular instance of it. In reading their base absurdities, one cannot but recollect the expression of Marshal Villars (I think it was) to Lewis XIV. 'Sire, je vais combattre vos ennemis, & je vous laisse au milieu des miens.'—Sir Arthur, much worse treated than M. de Villars, says nothing about it, but beats his country's enemies, and despises his own.

St. IX. l. 1. *But, tyrant, thou.* With all the reluctance which one must feel, to charge with atrocious crimes, a man whose transcendant talents (not always ill employed) have raised him to the highest station and power that any human being ever attained, it is yet impossible to think of his cruel and unprovoked attack on the Spanish crown and people without indignation—without feeling, that Divine justice must charge to his account, all the ruin by fire, famine and the sword, which his unparalleled injustice has visited upon that unhappy country.

St. IX. l. 20. *D'Enghien leads the shadowy crew.* The seizing the Duke D'Enghien in a neutral state, dragging him to a tribunal to which he was, in no view, amenable, condemning him by laws to which he owed no obedience, and finally putting him to death by a hasty, timid and illegal execution by *torch light*, are stains on Bonaparte's character, of such violence, injustice and cruelty, as no good fortune, no talents, no splendour of power, or even of merit, can ever obliterate.

St. X. l. 8. *England and Spain still brave thy power.* The author has never ventured to indulge any very sanguine hope of the final success of the Spanish cause, particularly since the retreat of the French from Madrid, and behind the Ebro, was turned to so little solid advantage by the Spaniards. But that their efforts and their example in a great degree crippled and distracted the power of France, and afforded a considerable chance for the emancipation of Europe ; that the victories of Baylen and Talavera, the defence of Saragossa and Gerona have been of great advantage (exclusive of any other) in dissipating the spell of French invincibility, cannot be denied. Undoubtedly Bonaparte will come out of the Spanish contest, even though he should succeed in placing his brother on the throne, with diminished reputation and more precarious power. It is singular that in the succession war a century ago, the French were obliged in like manner to retire from Madrid behind the Ebro, and that the negligence of the other party, in

not dislodging them from that position, eventually placed the
French competitor on the throne of Spain. *See Carleton's
Memoirs.*

St. XI. l. 17. *Ind's unequal war.* Sir Arthur Wellesley's campaign in India, was a masterpiece of courage and
conduct. At Assaye on the third of September, 1803, with
2,000 Europeans and 2,500 Native Troops he utterly defeated
the united armies of Scindia and the Rajah of Berar, amounting
(exclusive of a body of 20,000 cavalry) to at least 11,000
infantry ; strongly posted, furnished with a formidable and
well served train of artillery, and officered in a great degree
by French.

St. XIII. l. 12. *Wellesley undeceived.* The sagacity with
which Sir A. Wellesley always foresaw the enemy's point of
attack, and prepared means of repelling it, were very remarkable. Those modest gentlemen in England, who undervalue
his military abilities, are obliged (though unintentionally I
dare say) to deny at the same time those of *their friends* the
French, who admit that the English position was an excellent
one, and obstinately defended : but indeed this admission was
superfluous ; for the perseverance with which they assailed it,
sufficiently proves how important they thought it ! And let it
never be forgotten, that this position, five times at least at-
tacked with more than double forces by some of the best
generals and troops of France, was found to be impregnable.
But what are the opinions of the French Marshals, or even
the evidence of facts to the speculations of the tacticians of
Catherine Street, and the Strand ?

St. XIII. l. 20. *Commanding height.* Had the French succeeded in carrying that height on which General Hill's brigade alone was at first posted, but towards which Sir Arthur afterwards moved several other regiments, nothing, it is thought, could have saved the British and Spanish armies from an entire defeat.

St. XIV. l. 1. *Three columns.* Many of the circumstances of this and the next Stanza are taken from an excellent letter from an officer of the 48th to his friend in Dublin, which was published in the Freeman's Journal, of that city, of the 19th August, 1809.

St. XV. l. 32. *Langworth, and Albuquerque and Payne.* General Baron Langworth (who fell gloriously) commanded the German cavalry. The duke of Albuquerque was of considerable service with his corps of Spanish horse, and Generals Payne and Anson commanded the British cavalry. These troops brought off the remains of the 23d dragoons, who, in a charge headed by Colonel Seymour, had gotten entangled in a ravine and deep ditches, and were in danger of being entirely destroyed.—They behaved with great gallantry, but suffered a considerable loss, having however had the satisfaction of baffling Victor's (the duke of Belluno) attempt on General Hill's position.

St. XVI. l. 7. *Towards the centre.* The repulse of Victor by the dragoons, was followed by a general attack on the centre and right of the British line, which was every where gallantly repulsed ; but the action was severest towards the left of the centre, where General Sherbrook commanded : it was there that the gallant impetuosity of the Guards for a moment endangered the victory, and with the description of this principal attack the text is chiefly occupied.

St. XVIII. l. 18. *The flowing tide of victory turned.* It is not to be denied, that at this moment the fate of the day was something worse than doubtful, but Sir Arthur, as soon as he saw the advance of the Guards, anticipated the result, and moved other troops (among the rest the 48th regiment) from the heights into the plain, to cover the retreat, which took place as he expected.

St. XVIII. l. last. *Squanders himself away.* See the note on Stanza V. l. 14. Towards the close of the action, Sir A. Wellesley was struck by two balls (but without injury) and two of his Aid-de-camps were wounded at his side. On this occasion his personal exertions and peril seemed necessary to retrieve the victory.

St. XIX. l. 2. *A gallant legion.* The 48th regiment, by whose coolness and courage (and both were severely tried) the Guards were enabled to form again. Col. Donellan was unfortunately severely wounded at the head of this gallant corps.

St. XX. l. 5. *Desolating fires.* This circumstance is mentioned in private letters ; but not, that the French set fire to the field *designedly :*—it would rather seem that the accidental bursting of their shells in the dry grass occasioned this conflagration, which ravaged a great extent of ground, and entirely consumed many of the dead and (horrid to relate) some of the wounded. This must have been a new and striking feature of war.

St. **XXI.** l. 14. *France moves her busy bands.* Immediately after the repulse of their general attack, the French began to retire ; which they did in good order ; and during the night, effected their retreat towards Santa Olalla, leaving in the hands of the British 20 pieces of cannon, ammunition, tumbrils and prisoners.

St. **XXII.** l. 8. *For those that die*
            In honour's high career.

—I lament exceedingly that my plan and limits did not permit me to pay to some distinguished individuals who fell in this action, the tribute they deserved—but it is to be hoped, that the Country will show its sense of their glorious services and fall by a public monument.

FINIS.